Insane: Endorsements

'If you want to read Salvation Army history that's as exciting as a new day, then read this book. When we read what was achieved for social justice, and how the BIG issues were tackled with fervour and radical intelligence, we would be insane not to do the same today—and, believe me, there's more human slavery and more unresolved social justice issues today than in Booth's day.

'This book, written to challenge young Salvationists and written in fast-paced, mind-blowing language, will make a powerful impact on every reader. If you think history is dull and boring, this book will prove you wrong. But are we willing to be crazy enough to go out and make an impact for the Kingdom of God in our day, as Booth-Tucker or Bramwell Booth or W.T. Stead were in theirs? This book will inspire you to try!'

General Eva Burrows (Rtd)

'"INSANE"? Hardly. A fresh call to radical obedience and creative encounters with desperate human need could not be more timely. It is in our DNA as a movement. Fresh stimulus to live out our missional mandate can be found in this updated recall of Army responses to systemic evil and root causes of suffering and sin.'

General Paul A. Rader (Rtd)

'Insane is a "blow your mind" rendition of recklessly abandoned early pioneers who set about to change the world. Every Salvationist ought to read this book with a highlighter in hand and a notebook ready. For without a doubt, after your first read, passion will pump through your veins and charge you with holy enthusiasm and godly innovation to set some plans in motion yourself.'

Captain Danielle Strickland

'As a great man once said, "We stand on the shoulders of giants." By reading on, the present generation of Salvation Army innovators will see further into the future than ever before.'

Russell Rook

'This is a good one! Munn and Collinson effectively restate the meaning of our birthright, through stories that quicken the mind and stir the emotions. You can't read this without being challenged to "do something" for the kingdom—no matter the cost. Read it if you dare!'

Commissioner Israel Gaither

'I commend co-authors Nealson Munn and David Collinson for disinterring some of the stirring sagas and defining moments of Army history, and presenting them in a contemporary style and challenge. A must-read for every young Salvationist, and a refresher course for us veterans.'

Colonel Henry Gariepy (Rtd)

insane:

the stories of crazy salvos who changed the world

First published 2007

National Library of Australia
Cataloguing-in-Publication date 16 December 2007

Munn, Nealson Martin, 1985-; Collinson, David William, 1970-
Insane: the Stories of Crazy Salvos Who Changed the World
ISBN: 978-0-9585991-6-0
The Salvation Army – History. I. The Salvation Army. Australia Southern Territory. II. Title.

For Worldwide Distribution

This book and other Salvation Army resources are available at salvationarmy.org.au

Concept and 'Insane Challenges' by David Collinson
Stories by Nealson Munn
Design, layout and photography by Perri Winter (perriwinter@gmail.com)
Type set in Hot Pizza and Georgia

Subediting: The Salvation Army National Editorial Department, Australia
The Salvation Army, Australia Southern Territory, SALVO Publishing

Thanks to

Lindsay Cox (territorial archivist), Andrew Bertram Middleton (assistant to the territorial archivist), Major Laurie Robertson, Dawn Volz, Commissioners James and Carolyn Knaggs, Captains Stephen Court and Danielle Strickland, Perri Winter, Phil Wall, Lieutenant Sonia Jeffrey, Heather Power, Larry Reed, John Cleary, General Eva Burrows (Rtd), Lieutenants Genevieve Peterson and Catherine Shanks, Major Winsome Merrett and the illustrious denizens of the Corps Programme Department (especially the 2Love cubicle), Captain Kylie Collinson (and Noah and Josiah), Majors Richard and Janet Munn, Olivia Munn, Marcel Proust and our faithful comrades at Shop 16, Collingwood Outpost, Box Hill Citadel, the ROOTS Global Network and the Aggressive Christianity Conference. You are all INSANE!

Foreword

'Tell me the old, old story...'

I can still remember listening to this age-old hymn being sung by lovely but warbling old ladies at the home league. The poet calls to others to tell them the story of faith, the one that has inspired countless millions to surrender their lives for the sake of the King and His Kingdom; the story of life and hope that has brought salvation to the world, the story of Jesus doing what He does best—changing people's lives, working through His people, to transform the world.

That story is what this book is all about.

The Salvation Army was raised on a diet of faith-filled risk and outrageous innovation. The stories contained within this book are a feast of those early adventures that made such an impact upon the world and endeared the 'Salvos' to the hearts of communities around the globe. Booth's 'war on two fronts' theology and mission philosophy set a platform for Salvationists to assert, with what was almost a form of divine arrogance, that there was not one sphere of life, not a place on this planet, where injustice and ungodliness could or should be tolerated or remain unchallenged. Their tool kit was filled with courage, creativity, rigorous engagement and understanding of the issues of the day, and an insane level of innovation.

Munn and Collinson have done us a great service in capturing the essence of these Salvo heroes and their stories, to remind us again of the rich legacy that is waiting to be inherited by their modern-day descendants. A new generation of young radicals is emerging within the Salvation Army; they are creating, initiating, challenging the status quo, provoking, annoying, experimenting—demonstrating some distinctly insane behaviours, and they are feeling very much at home with the Salvos, for this legacy is theirs.

The remarkable challenges of the third millenium require new conversations between men and women of faith who are infused with the creative genius of the Divine Innovator and have the courage to ignite these ideas with the passion and sacrifice required.

This book will pour fuel on the fires of their insanity—long may they burn.

Phil Wall

London

12 December 2007

introduction:

'To better the future we must disturb the present.'
Catherine Booth

W hen writing a book such as this—that is, a book that attempts to make old stories interesting to a new generation of readers—one is tempted to begin with some palpitating dramatisation.

> A tall, bearded stranger with piercing eyes and an acutely sloping pseudo-Semitic nose strode boldly down Mile End Road, his lithe body wrapped in a black trench coat. Lifting a frail but well-formed finger to heaven, he intoned in a gravelly baritone, with a faint Midlands accent: 'There is a Heaven in East London for everyone who will look to Christ as Saviour!'

> Jeers, pebbles and bottles flew from a nearby pub—but a grimy face pressed to one of the windows registered recognition. It was the venerable publican himself, who quietly murmured, 'Why, that be Will Booth o' Sneinton, or my name's not Old Jack Shandy!' His fingers drummed restlessly against the glass pane. Biting his lower lip, he remarked ruefully, as though addressing the dank, boozy air, 'These blokes don't know what they're up against...'

Alternatively, one might adopt a highbrow tone from the start, in order to winnow the scholarly cream from the casual-reader chaff.

> 'Through stories,' wrote novelist Leslie Marmon Silko, 'we hear who we are.' In our age it has become common in intellectual circles to regard all discourse in terms of stories, not just in the field of literature but also in disciplines traditionally viewed as theoretical or scientific, such as

theology—which now encompasses an entire school of 'narrative' theology—and even physics, in which the way we represent to ourselves a phenomenon such as the atom may be thought of as a kind of story...

Others will favour a more direct, personal approach.

If you're like me, growing up as a Salvationist you probably found yourself a trifle bewildered. Why did the mention of Commissioner Andrew Miller always send the little old bonneted lady in the front pew into ecstasies? Why did the spectacle of your corps officer draping a flag around himself and shouting 'Hiss if you dare!' cause laughter to ripple across the congregation? What is meant by 'the Cab Horse Charter'? Well, now your confusion is over: in this book we've set out to put such questions to rest!

But let us instead begin with a word about the title—*Insane: The Stories of Crazy Salvos Who Changed the World*. This says something about both the book and its subject. What you are reading is a collection of stories, all of which have been told before, but none, we believe, in quite this way. Until now they have existed primarily in dusty volumes with obscure titles like *The Heavenly Witch* or *Booth-Tucker: Sadhu and Saint*. Without such works this one would never have come into being; but, while acknowledging our debt to these classics, we recognise that few modern readers are willing to plod through a Booth biography of *War and Peace* dimensions, especially one written in prose that proclaims its 19th century vintage with every phrase. Our aim, then, is to preserve and promote The Salvation Army's heritage of innovation by retelling its classic stories in a manner that will interest and inspire contemporary Salvationists.

These stories concern two things: (1) crazy Salvos, and (2) their innovations. The mildly provocative title *Insane* is a description applied to many Salvationists, correctly or incorrectly, as well as a kind of acronym—INSANE: INnovative SAlvationists' NEtwork (a bit of a stretch, granted, but we think it works). What sort of 'network' is this? It is one that extends backwards to The Salvation Army's founders, William and Catherine Booth, and forwards, as it is carried into the future by Salvationists of today. Its members include evangelists, reformers, renegades, journalists, renegade journalists, magistrates-turned-beggars, reformed prostitutes, entrepreneurs, nurses, doughnut dealers and pop stars. It comprises teenagers and octogenarians, men and women, westerners and easterners—with surnames ranging from Booth and Tucker to Weerasooriya and Garabedian.

This book charts the development of INSANE from the founding of The Christian Mission (later to become The Salvation Army) in 1865 to the emergence of the Joystrings, the first Salvationist rock group, 100 years later. Most of what we recount occurred before 1900—the Army's first few decades were too explosive to short-change. With a bit more scholarly acumen, however, one could easily compile a companion volume doing justice to Salvation Army innovations in the 20th century and beyond. In fact, we believe that the greater part of the INSANE story has yet to be written. This book has as much to do with your life as it has to do with Salvation Army history. That is why we added an 'INSANE Challenge' at the end of every chapter—to make explicit the challenge that the life of each Salvo innovator implicitly offers us.

To the question 'What has The Salvation Army of yesterday to do with us today?' we reply in the words of George Orwell: 'But then, what have you in common with the child of five whose photograph your mother keeps on the mantelpiece? Nothing, except that you happen to be the same person.' Today's Salvation Army 'happens to be' the same army that successfully agitated for the raising of England's age of consent, that invaded India with bare feet and beggars' bowls, and that promoted women to leadership roles even though the established churches vigorously protested.

In the first act of Shakespeare's *The Tempest* we read: 'What seest thou else in the dark backward and abysm of time?' As you gaze into the 'dark backward and abysm' of Salvation Army history, you may, in fact, find yourself overwhelmed by the radiant brightness of what you see. But don't shut your eyes: instead, let the lives of these 'crazy Salvos' shed light on the problems of today's world that require daring, innovative solutions, and then— go and do likewise.

chapter one:

Mile End Waste:

*How William and Catherine Booth took
the gospel from the sanctuary to the street*

'The commencement of The Salvation Army, as the General
himself would admit, was on Mile End Waste.'
The Mining World, December 1906

Perhaps the greatest innovation in Salvation Army history was The Salvation Army itself. We refer not to the movement's military structure—its sprawling, teeming apparatus of epaulets, crests, caps, pins, drums, flags, ranks, cartridges, enrolments, marching orders, promotions and the like—but simply to its aggressive posture: while traditional churches resided, The Salvation Army invaded. Traditional churches clung to the sanctuary; The Salvation Army identified itself as a 'church of the back street'.

To illustrate the point, we may consider the early ministry of Catherine Booth. Whereas most churchwomen in the 1860s balked at sharing a theatre box with an adulteress, let alone entering the home of a prostitute, Catherine routinely preached in London brothels. A witness to one such sermon was struck by Catherine's empathy with her audience: 'She identified herself with them as a fellow sinner, showing that if they supposed her to be better than themselves it was a mistake, since all had sinned against God.'

A deep compassion for the plight of society's outcasts, combined with the boldness and initiative to visit them on their home turf, was not just a distinctive of The Salvation Army—it was its very essence.

Today, the legendary status of the Army's most prolific innovators, William and Catherine Booth, is secure. Christians of all varieties draw inspiration from their lives, and even secular observers find them admirable: 'As human beings they were remarkable by any standards,' writes British politician Roy Hattersley; 'they deserve a place in the pantheon of Great Victorians.' Within Army circles, of course, they are even more exalted—role models, intellectual authorities, exemplars of Salvationism *par excellence*. Among the highest and most delicate compliments one Salvationist can pay to another is: 'The Founder would approve.' Conversely, the Salvationist's most damning accusation is: 'William Booth must be turning in his grave.' In most Salvation Army meeting halls one or both of the Founders may be seen gazing sternly upon all that transpires—a favourite portrait being one of William in old age, resting his cheek against his knuckles with an expression of extreme fatigue—a reflection, perhaps, of the enormous labour he expended in the long, hard task of founding The Salvation Army.

William was born in Sneinton, a village of Nottingham, England, on 10 April 1829. His father, a builder, fell into financial ruin in 1842 and died only months later, leaving the 13-year-old to provide for the family. William reluctantly enrolled as a pawnbroker's apprentice. Like other eminent Victorians—Charles Dickens, for example—he was to grow up in an environment of poverty and misery. But while he dreaded his occupation, there was light amidst the darkness. Two years into his apprenticeship, he 'had the advantage of hearing some good preaching' and 'came under the influence of some godly companions'. Believing himself truly saved for the first time, he abandoned his father's Anglicanism and joined the Wesleyan Methodists.

WHY CAN'T I KEEP MY BIG IDEAS TO MYSELF!

Even the best officers have their 'off days'. Human qualities are what we look for in young Candidates. Have you got what it takes to carry on with the 'big idea'?

It's the longest, hardest most satisfying job in the Army Can you be an Officer?

1980s Australian officers' recruitment poster.

Within 10 years, William became an itinerant preacher with the Methodists, and was renowned for his arresting oratory. It was in this capacity that he first caught the attention of Miss Catherine Mumford, a strict Methodist born in the same year as him. She mentioned her admiration of the young preacher's forceful style to his patron, Edward Rabbits, and Rabbits proposed a tea party. The guest list would include William, Catherine and himself.

The conversation at this historic first meeting concerned the evils of drink. William made an egregious *faux pas* by admitting that he was not a teetotaller (at age seven a classmate had persuaded him to sign a pledge of total and eternal abstinence from alcohol, but in adulthood he recanted and 'took intoxicants in moderation'—for health). Catherine argued passionately for prohibition. Although William's immediate response is uncertain, at a later time, certainly, he was to adopt Catherine's views on this point (and, as we shall see, this was not the only opinion she imparted to him). William met Catherine again at a Good Friday service on 10 April 1852—a landmark day for young William, as it was also his 23rd birthday, the day his apprenticeship ended and his career as a full-time preacher began. After the service Miss Mumford felt ill, and William kindly escorted her home. The Mumfords insisted that he spend the night at their house rather than trek across London to his own lodgings.

It was the beginning of what William later described as 'an exceptional union of hearts and purpose of life'.

They were engaged that same year, and the marriage took place on 16 June 1855. Their first child, Bramwell, was born less than a year later (William described him as 'a plump, round faced, dark complexioned, black pated little fellow'). In 1858 William was ordained as a minister with the Methodist New Connexion, one of the many revivalistic movements in England at that time. However, unhappy with the various constraints the denomination imposed, William resigned not long afterwards, exchanging the security of Methodist affiliation for the possibility of reaching a broader audience.

Meanwhile, a momentous transformation occurred that would have profound ramifications for the Booth family. In 1860, Catherine Booth began preaching.

She was a great success from the start. The sheer novelty of a woman preaching was an important element of her appeal—sometimes her sermons were advertised: 'Come and hear a woman preach'. On the other hand, without her innate charisma Catherine's preaching career could never have been as successful as it was.

A *Wesleyan Times* report of the mid-1860s attempts to convey her unique stage presence. She wore 'a black loose fine jacket with loose sleeves, which appeared exceedingly suitable to her while preaching', and she had 'a rather prepossessing countenance'. As to her delivery, it was 'calm and precise,' her manner 'quiet' and marked by an 'entire absence

The young revivalists.

13

of unbecoming confidence'—all of which suggested a woman of 'no ordinary mind'. For a time, she was the most sought after evangelist in the Booth family, attracting such large crowds and winning so many converts that she was invited to tour the entire Methodist circuit in London. William, with admirable humility, remained in the north of England with the children—there were six by this time, out of an eventual total of eight.

All the Booth children survived to adulthood, an exception in those days, but several were plagued with health problems and emotional instability. Some observers wondered if this resulted from Catherine's frequent absence. The publishers of *The Revival*, a magazine the Booths depended upon for publicity and financial support, wrote to William questioning 'whether it is right for mothers of families to be away from home duties'. They failed to recognise that Catherine was, at that time, the breadwinner of the household. While William toiled in the country, she was creating a sensation in London. It was an unusual arrangement, and there is no telling how long it might have persisted had William not been offered a six-week preaching engagement in East London—by, of all people, the publishers of *The Revival*. Although he did not know it, he was about to embark upon the great work of his life.

The years since his departure from the Methodist New Connection had been difficult for William. Despite the joys of his growing family and Catherine's remarkable success, it was a trial to leave the comforts of an established movement for the rigours of independent preaching. However, his son Bramwell suggests that this was an important time of preparation for the young revivalist. 'This period, dark and perplexing as it was, was a period in which, I consider, he was being most marvellously fitted for the work which, unknown to him, was awaiting his hand in the East End of London.'

What precisely awaited Booth in the East End? As readers of Dickens will know, it was not a pleasant place in the mid-19th century. Sir Walter Besant goes so far as to claim that there was 'no other city in the world in the least like East London for the unparalleled magnitude of its meanness'. The district simply lacked the infrastructure to support its burgeoning population. 'Nothing in the city was equipped to cope,' writes historian Henry Chadwick. 'Municipal government, building, sanitation, health, cemeteries, hospitals, roads, paving, lighting, police, dentists, schools—all the organs of city life were strained till they were bursting.' The disturbance of trade caused by the American Civil War had led to an increase in unemployment, and without basic amenities to alleviate the hardships of urban life—which for most people meant working long hours in unsafe conditions for little pay—the denizens of East London turned to vice.

It did not help that the British Parliament, acting on the belief that making beer more readily available would reduce the consumption of spirits, had in 1830 removed the beer tax and facilitated an easier distribution of beer and cider. Sales of beer quickly increased, those of spirits did not decrease, and alcoholism became rampant in the East End. Salvation Army historian Robert Sandall asserts: 'The prevailing drinking habits of the people formed a wretched background to every other misery, and were indeed the cause of a very great deal of it.'

The Salvation Army arose against this grim backdrop, but it did not do so alone: happily, the emerging Victorian humanitarian movement was helping to lighten the heavy circumstances. It was an age when the spirit of reform pervaded both sacred and secular circles, with the interesting result that radical religion and progressive politics found themselves engaged in similar tasks—a unique confluence that would determine the eventual direction of the Booths' ministry.

Arriving in the East End in the summer of 1865, William Booth did not expect to succeed. Although today we chiefly associate him with the city of London, he was raised in a small village, and most of his ministry until that point (he was then 36 years old) had taken place in rural areas. Slum-dwellers intimidated him. 'I feared my ability to deal with people of this class,' he later told George Scott Railton. At heart, he was still a country boy.

However, the sight of the East End's desolation wrung his heart. There was, most obviously, the physical privation of the neighbourhood, which has been vividly depicted by biographer Richard Collier:

> If the cheese was tinted with red lead to simulate high-priced red Double Gloucester, the poor would not complain. In the same way they accepted other adulterations: street-sold lemonade spiked with oil of vitriol, flour doctored with pipe-clay, cocoa gritty with earth. When two farthings could unbalance a weekly budget, none dared set too high a store on quality.

Just as apparent to William Booth, however, was the neighbourhood's spiritual decay. 'In every direction,' he wrote, 'were multitudes totally ignorant of the Gospel and given up to all kinds of wickedness—infidels, drunkards, thieves, harlots, gamblers, blasphemers and pleasure seekers without number.'

Booth made the courageous decision to hold open-air meetings on the 'Mile End Waste,' an area of undeveloped land along Mile End Road (so named because the two public houses near its terminus lay exactly one mile from Aldgate, where the road began). Here, in Sandall's words, 'shows, shooting-ranges, petty dealers, and quack doctors rivalled one another in attracting the attention of passers-by'. It was an unattractive setting, to say the least, and its twin pubs, 'The Blind Beggar' and 'The Vines', were notorious. Booth expected that his mission to the Mile End Waste would be nothing more than 'a very short salvation campaign'. Later, however, he recognised it as the beginning of his great work. Nevertheless, it was a humble beginning. In 1904 he recalled: 'My field of labour was the Mile End; my tabernacle, an old tent in a disused burying-ground; my audience, a crowd of poor Whitechapellers; and the result—blessed be God—was a few desolate souls at the mercy seat.'

From 'a few desolate souls,' the nightly tent meetings grew to attract sizable crowds. A jubilant correspondent to *The Revival* expressed his appreciation for William's ministry:

> I am very happy to inform you that the Lord has been with us at the Tent this week, and has blessed the labours of our dear Brother Booth. On Sunday, 2nd July, after our brother's address, many stayed behind to be spoken to about Jesus. Four professed to find peace in believing and two backsliders were restored.

Booth was so effective that he was invited to stay longer than six weeks. On 20 August the *Wesleyan Times* ran an article on his flourishing campaign:

> The Rev. William Booth has been engaged for the past seven weeks holding a series of special meetings in the East End of London near the London Hospital and in the Mile End Road. Hundreds of working men and numbers of persons who never enter any place of worship have listened night after night to appeals of this devoted servant of God, and many conversions have taken place. The work is assuming a permanent character and a large hall in the neighbourhood is about to be engaged for the winter...In no part of the Metropolis is there greater need for an evangelistic effort.

Of course, the work was not without its difficulties. In addition to the indifference and insolence of the 'working men,' Booth had also to contend with the hostility of the publicans, who feared a decline in business as a result of his ministry. Their operations were by no means secure, and the loss of a few devoted patrons was a severe blow. There was also an unfortunate partnership between the publicans and the police, who often watched complacently as hired roughs abused Booth and his fellow evangelists.

Still, Booth was finding the experience intensely rewarding. His initial plans for temporary residency morphed into a tenuous attachment, which in turn morphed into total commitment. Returning home late one night after a meeting at Mile End Waste, he declared to Catherine: 'Darling, I have found my destiny.'

Mrs Booth hesitated for only a moment, initially concerned that a permanent engagement in the East End would alienate William's patrons in the country, leaving their family without means of support. Perhaps she sensed the urgency and appropriateness of William's calling; in any event, her acquiescence was a step of faith rather than a rationally informed decision: 'If you feel you ought to stay...stay!' she replied; 'we have trusted the Lord once for our support, and we can trust him again.'

Sure enough, within days of the decision to stay in East London, William received an invitation to visit Samuel Morley, a wealthy manufacturer and philanthropist intrigued by the Mile End mission. At their interview Morley raised the question of the support of the Booth family, and suggested that he and some of his friends would be willing to provide it. Interestingly, it was particularly Booth's courage in the face of persecution that impressed Morley. Frederick Booth-Tucker mentions the philanthropist's sympathy for 'the open-air meetings on the Mile End Waste, surrounded by the blaspheming infidels and boisterous drunkards' and 'the processions down the Whitechapel road, pelted with garbage'. In harassing William Booth, the publicans had unwittingly provided his means of remaining in the East End.

Thus 1865 saw the founding of the Christian Mission, later to become The Salvation Army. From his initial attitude of zeal dampened by self-doubt—

> I would have given worlds, had they been mine, to have been qualified to attract and interest and then lead to Salvation the masses I saw around me...but I despaired of accomplishing it. This I thought was not my vocation.

—William Booth had matured into a highly effective urban evangelist. Now, with the charismatic Catherine joining him in the East End, the Booths would establish the pattern of ministry—and the tough indifference to persecution—that they maintained throughout their careers.

The original innovation of taking the gospel from the Methodist meeting hall to the Mile End Waste was carried to creative extremes. In 1867, for example, William preached a sermon outside 'The Blind Beggar', adopting the tavern's name, derived from an old English children's fable, as his theme. Hundreds of inebriated, nostalgic men came to hear the childhood favourite retold. 'My mother', one convert recollected, 'often told me when a lad about the blind beggar of Bethnal Green. Thinks I, I would like to hear that tale again, I'll go and hear him. But lo and behold, when I got there, it was me that was the blind beggar!'

Through such tactics, the Booths reached audiences who would never have approached the doors of a traditional church. The Salvation Army's tradition of innovation had begun.

Insane Challenge:

The decision to take the gospel from the sanctuary to the street was original and edgy. It was a desperate bid—and a clever strategy—to share Christ with thousands of people who would never enter a church.

Are we still seeking out the places where the poor and disadvantaged reside? Do we still direct our resources and energy toward these people?

Today many of us seem content merely to copy other popular ministry approaches, but what made the primitive Salvation Army unique was its mission to the last, the lost and the least. We must identify the people that God has called us to reach and then adapt our methods in order to reach them. Often, we do the reverse: we employ certain established methods regardless of the mission we are trying to achieve.

Aside from its originality, a further characteristic of the early Army was its boldness. Do we still have the confidence to challenge today's 'publicans'? We must not be afraid to confront evil wherever it resides. We should be proactive regarding such places, and should assist those who have been hurt by pubs and gambling venues.

William Booth found his destiny in ministry to the poor and marginalised. His next step was to engage others to help him and support him financially. Are we bold enough to believe that God will provide for us when we step out in faith, or do we only step out once all finances and personnel are secure?

Here is a 'Mile End Guide' for starting Salvation Army work in your area:

1. Ask God to give you a heart for the lost, the last and the least.

2. Locate the poor and marginalised in your town or city.

3. Find creative means of taking the gospel to those people, rather than expecting them to come to you.

4. Step out in faith: as you begin ministry, trust God to help you in matters of finance and personnel.

5. Regardless of opposition, stand up for the oppressed.

chapter two:

My Best Men Are Women:

How female leaders shaped
The Salvation Army

> **'Miss Mumford scorned the notion that a minister's wife was to content herself with being a mere ornamental appendage to her husband, a figure-head to grace his tea-table...'**
> *Frederick Booth-Tucker*

In The Salvation Army's early years William Booth wrote a series of *Orders and Regulations for Officers* that today seem both old-fashioned and remarkably progressive. The *Orders and Regulations for Field Officers*, for example, places comically detailed, austere strictures on daily life—'Suppers, as a rule, are bad; but when Officers take an early tea, especially when a good deal of work is done afterwards, some light refreshment will be needed before going to bed. In which case a little hot milk poured over a little bread is handy and will be found nourishing, soothing, and agreeable to the palate, and favourable to sleep.'

Other passages have aged more gracefully, especially a chapter in the *Orders and Regulations for Staff Officers* that still strikes us as a revolutionary statement on the role of women in a religious organisation:

One of the leading principles upon which The Army is based is the right of woman to an equal share with man in the great work of publishing Salvation to the world...Let it therefore be understood that women are eligible for the highest Commands—indeed, no woman is to be kept back from any position of power or influence merely on account of her sex.

These principles were published under William Booth's name, but they were most likely written at Catherine Booth's request. On the issue of female ministry Catherine was both ahead of her husband and ahead of her time. As early as 1855, 10 years before the founding of the Christian Mission, 'Miss Mumford' wrote to a hesitant William, then her fiancé, urging him to form a decided opinion on the role of women in the church: 'Let me advise you, my Love, to get settled views on this subject.'

Her own are abundantly clear. 'I believe that one of the greatest boons to the race would be woman's exaltation to her proper position, mentally and spiritually,' she proclaims, even going so far as to add, 'What endears the Christian religion to my heart is what it *has done, and is destined* to do, for my own sex.' Though William's vacillation today seems less admirable than Catherine's principled zeal, in context it is understandable. What his fiancée suggested was scarcely short of heresy by the standards of the 19th century. Catherine Booth's views would offend many churchmen today; to those of her Victorian milieu, they were positively scandalous.

Her opinions were not formed in a vacuum—the American holiness teacher Phoebe Palmer, for example, exerted a powerful influence on Catherine's thought. Still, Catherine was precociously forward-thinking: Palmer defended women's ministry in her 1859 book *The Promise of the Father*, but Catherine's *Female Ministry* appeared in the same year; Palmer was 52 years old, Catherine only 30.

insane: chapter two:

Decades earlier, a few secular voices had spoken for women's rights. In the late 18th and early 19th centuries, strong female thinkers, such as Mary Wollstonecraft, and strong male advocates for women's rights, such as John Stuart Mill, began to achieve prominence in intellectual circles. Nevertheless, in the late 1800s women were generally viewed as passionate, beautiful, but ultimately rather limited and silly creatures, whose role in public life ought to be rigidly circumscribed. Virginia Woolf elucidates the paradox of this stereotype—'The spirit of life and beauty in a kitchen chopping up suet.'

It was startling, then, for Catherine to challenge not only her husband's views, but those of other prominent men in her community, such as the Reverend David Thomas, a Congregationalist minister to whom she addressed a letter of more than 1200 words, complaining—and carefully arguing—against his preaching on the moral and spiritual inferiority of women. The letter reveals not only Catherine's passionate opinions on women's equality but, just as importantly, her ability to marshal biblical arguments in support of her views.

Interestingly, the letter was sent unsigned—not, it seems clear, because Catherine refused to own her beliefs, but in order to protect her husband's career. At the time William was associated with the Methodist church, and lacked the autonomy he would gain when he and Catherine left to form their own mission. By that time William's opinions had solidified. At first a reluctant supporter, he finally became an enthusiastic proponent of Catherine's views. While General of The Salvation Army he famously declared: 'Some of my best men are women.' William tended to reach his opinions intuitively. As a young man, he read a

'The Army Mother': Catherine Booth.

Calvinist text in order to broaden his theological horizons, but was so infuriated by the doctrine of predestination that he hurled the book against a wall after only one paragraph. Catherine, on the other hand, grounded her views in rigorous argument and compendious knowledge, so that, on an issue on which William was uncertain and Catherine decided, it was only a matter of time before the General capitulated.

Perhaps because her husband now concurred with her views, perhaps because she foresaw that his departure from the Methodists was inevitable, by 1859 Catherine Booth did not hesitate to take credit for her ideas. Gone were the days of her unsigned letters: in *Female Ministry* she openly professed that women's preaching is edifying to the church and entirely sanctioned by the Bible. This position set her against the spirit of her age. A remark of Samuel Johnson's reveals the condescension still prevalent in Catherine's time: 'A woman's preaching is like a dog's walking on his hinder legs. It is not done well, but you are surprised to find it done at all.' Of course, many churchmen believed that a woman's preaching was not only surprising, but also unbiblical and wrong.

Female Ministry, then, was a revolutionary document, anticipating several later feminist ideas, chief among them the argument that observable inferiorities in women are the product of culture rather than nature. Regarding public speaking, for example, Catherine wrote:

> We must admit that want of mental culture, the trammels of custom, the force of prejudice, and one-sided interpretations of Scripture, have hitherto almost excluded her from this sphere;

but before such a sphere is pronounced to be unnatural, it must be proved either that woman has not the ability to teach or to preach or that the possession and exercise of this ability unnaturalises her in other respects.

Virginia Woolf, an icon of feminism, echoed this idea 70 years later in her essay *A Room of One's Own*, which considers the dearth of female writers in European literature—'It is a perennial puzzle why no woman wrote a word of that extraordinary literature when every other man, it seemed, was capable of song or sonnet.' She argues that intellectual freedom depends upon material prosperity, so that, owing to their inferior social position throughout history, women 'have not had a dog's chance of writing poetry'. In other words, it is the 'trammels of custom' that exclude women from literary achievement.

Unlike Woolf, however, Catherine Booth was concerned to show that feminine achievement is not only natural but biblical—hence her claim that woman's exclusion from preaching arises not only from the 'trammels of custom' but also from 'one-sided interpretations of scripture'. A bold claim, for Catherine's conservative Wesleyanism required that she regard all scripture as 'the divine rule of faith and practice' (the formulation of The Salvation Army's first doctrine); she could not, for example, discredit such verses as 1 Timothy 2:12: 'But I suffer not a woman to teach, nor to usurp authority over the man, but to be in silence.'

Audaciously, Catherine purported to show that, taken as a whole, the Bible suggests equality between men and women. Were the opposite true, she maintains, her own views would differ accordingly. She considers the popular argument that female ministry is forbidden by scripture:

> This is by far the most serious objection which we have to consider—and if capable of substantiation, should receive our immediate and cheerful acquiescence; but we think that we shall be able to show, by a fair and consistent interpretation, that the very opposite view is the truth; that not only is the public ministry of woman unforbidden, but absolutely enjoined by both precept and example in the Word of God.

To this end, she undertakes a careful refutation of the thesis that women must be forbidden to speak in church, analysing the logic of Paul's epistles (especially 1 Timothy 2:12 and 1 Corinthians 11:4–5) with reference to 'eminent Greek scholars'. She also reaches back to the Old Testament to support her case, citing God's promise in the Book of Joel: 'And it shall come to pass afterward, that I will pour out my spirit upon all flesh; and your sons and your daughters shall prophesy, your old men shall dream dreams, your young men shall see visions: And also upon the servants and upon the handmaids in those days will I pour out my spirit.'

To commentators who say, 'If women have the gift of prophecy, they must not use that gift in public,' Catherine retorts, 'But God says, by His prophet Joel, they *shall* use it, just in the same sense as the sons use it.' She next reaches outside of scripture, citing references to female ministry in Justin Martyr and Iraneaus. On the whole, however, she criticises the church fathers as 'slow to accept' the ministry of women—a mistake with consequences as pernicious as those of any heresy. Catherine places those who oppose female ministry in the same class as those who support Universalism, Antinomianism, and Unitarianism ('that soul-withering doctrine'). Still, her conclusion is optimistic: 'Thank God the day is dawning with respect to this subject.' She even hazards a prophecy of her own:

> When the true light shines and God's works take the place of man's traditions, the doctor of divinity who shall teach that Paul commands woman to be silent when God's Spirit urges her to speak, will be regarded much the same as we should regard an astronomer who should teach that the sun is the earth's satellite.

The 'true light', it seems, has yet to shine, for the scriptural interpretations Catherine endorsed are still a subject of heated debate; nevertheless, the overall argument of *Female Ministry* has proven decisive in the development of The Salvation Army. For Salvationists and non-Salvationists alike, *Female Ministry* remains a challenging document to this day.

✦ ✦ ✦

Happily, Catherine was not alone in her crusade against women's subordination. Besides her husband, she had a powerful ally in the person of George Scott Railton, a friend, comrade and frequent house guest of the Booths, who played an important role in the formation of the Army's theology. The son of Wesleyan missionaries, Railton was converted at age 10, orphaned at 15 (his parents died of cholera during a mission to the Isle of Man), and at 19, penniless, homeless and jobless, he left London to Christianise Africa. He intended to reach 'some unknown part of Africa to which no missionary had penetrated', but instead found himself stranded in Morocco. This laudable effort having failed, he returned to England two years later to work in his uncle's shipping company.

His association with The Salvation Army began in 1872 when he read a publication from the Christian Mission, *How to Reach the Masses with the Gospel*. He was so impressed that he sent William Booth a letter volunteering his service. He became William's first lieutenant within a year, five years before the mission was rechristened The Salvation Army.

As an outspoken advocate of female leadership, it was fitting that Railton should take seven women with him when he departed in 1880 to start a mission in New York City. He and the 'Hallelujah Lassies' arrived safely after 26 days at sea, and within a year had won 1,500 converts. Railton established an additional Army operation in Newark, New Jersey, and, ever ambitious, had begun a mission in St Louis, Missouri when William Booth called him back to England in 1881.

The work in New York City was strengthened by an unofficial mission already founded in Philadelphia. This earlier work was fruit of the precocious initiative and dedication of 16-year-old Eliza Shirley, who became a lieutenant in 1879, shortly before her family immigrated to America. As an officer, Eliza required a special dispensation to leave her appointment in England. She wrote to General Booth to suggest that she start a mission in Philadelphia. With uncharacteristic caution, he replied, 'Start it on the principles of The Salvation Army, and if it is a success we may see our way to take it over.'

Upon arriving in Philadelphia, Eliza and her mother searched for a hall in which to hold Salvation Army meetings. They found a derelict furniture factory and persuaded the owner to let it for $10 a month. Christening the new outpost 'The Salvation Factory', they set out to refurbish the building, plugging holes in the roof, replacing broken windowpanes and covering the dirt floor with sawdust. Although they had left England because of financial desperation, Eliza's father borrowed money to purchase wood for benches and a platform.

The final step was to advertise around the neighbourhood:

Blood and Fire! The Salvation Army
Two Hallelujah females
will speak and sing for Jesus
in the old chair factory

Twelve people attended the inaugural 'Salvation Factory' service. The first Salvation Army meeting to be held in the United States began coolly, but intensified when a notorious drunkard was converted. Soon the Shirleys' work in Philadelphia was firmly established— it was, in fact, news of their success that decided Railton on his expedition to New York. A London *War Cry* in 1880 presented the Philadelphian triumph as a divine mandate:

WE MUST GO! This news has come upon us like a voice from Heaven and leaves us no choice. Mr. Railton must for a time postpone his North Wales expedition in order to take command of a force with which he hopes to sail about 13th February for New York, and the United States must, throughout their length and breadth, be overrun by Salvation desperadoes.[1]

In the same year that Railton and the 'Hallelujah Lassies' sailed for New York, William and Catherine Booth's eldest daughter launched The Salvation Army in Paris. Twenty-two-year-old Kate Booth led a team of two lieutenants (including 19-year-old Florence Soper, future wife of Bramwell Booth), conducting open-air meetings in the populous and notorious Parisian district of Belleville. Their French was embarrassing—the first French Salvation Army flag, hand-sewn by Catherine Booth, awkwardly translated the slogan 'Blood and Fire' as 'Du Sang et Du Feu' (a simple 'Sang et Feu' would have sufficed, and was later adopted). No doubt this contributed to the hostile reception Kate and her lieutenants received. While preaching, they were not only mocked, but pelted with mud and stones. On more than one occasion local drunks attempted to strangle the young lieutenants with their own bonnet strings, so that eventually the women attached the strings with pins rather than stitches. In a country not generally known for its hospitality, The Salvation Army received an especially harsh welcome. 'If I cannot save France,' Kate Booth resolved, 'I can at least die for it.'

This determination produced results. There were 100 converts in the first year, 500 in the second, and numerous officers and soldiers enrolled. Paris's animosity finally

---

1. *The hyperbolic, almost jocular tone of much early Salvationist rhetoric was deliberate. Although 'Primitive' Salvationists took their mission seriously, their jargon was treated lightly, as a flexible vehicle for creative communication.*

turned to respect, and Kate Booth was exalted as 'La Maréchale' (The Marshal), a title she bore for the rest of her life.

An even more storied leader is Evangeline Booth, fourth daughter of William and Catherine, who is to the history of The Salvation Army what Queen Elizabeth I is to the history of England. Both were unmarried women famed for their boldness: Elizabeth once said: 'I have the body of a weak and feeble woman, but the heart and stomach of a king!'; Evangeline, hissed at during an early Salvation Army meeting in the United States, wrapped herself in the American flag and challenged the audience: 'Hiss if you dare!' At another meeting, wounded when a sharp stone struck her arm, she accosted the man who had thrown it, brandishing her bleeding limb and demanding, 'Bandage this, quick! You did it, you fix it!' The man obeyed, and later joined The Salvation Army.

'Eva is the orator of the family,' William Booth noted, after hearing his 10-year-old daughter expound the theme 'God is love' to a rapt audience of dolls, brooms and cushions. In a family of eight children—including the charismatic Ballington Booth, known to twist diabolical horns in his hair while preaching about the devil—this was no small compliment. Evangeline held one of the longest leadership terms of any woman in The Salvation Army, serving as Commander in Canada for eight years, Commander in the United States for 30 years, and General of The Salvation Army for five years. She was the first female General, but not the last—another Eva, General Eva Burrows, was elected in 1986, and would serve as General for seven years.

✦ ✦ ✦

In a phrase dear to the hearts many feminists, Virginia Woolf declared, 'We think back through our mothers if we are women'. Similarly, if we are Salvationists, we cannot but think back through our mothers, for The Salvation Army has been guided by women, both intellectually and pragmatically, ever since it began. The ideas of Catherine Booth, for example, not only influence 'Salvationism' as conceived today, but constitute its very

The General with his seventh child, 'the orator of the family'.

substance. At a time when professors were still delivering lectures on 'The Mental, Moral, and Physical Inferiority of the Female Sex', The Salvation Army acknowledged 'the right of woman to an equal share with man in the great work of publishing Salvation to the world', a statement that remains an indispensable distinctive of the movement, and one of its most daring innovations.

Evangeline knew the value of a striking image.

Insane Challenge:

Female leadership has always been a distinctive characteristic of The Salvation Army—indeed, many people maintain that it was women who truly launched our movement. While most Victorian churches prevented females from exercising gifts such as preaching and administration, Catherine Booth forged a theology of biblical egalitarianism and co-founded a mission intended to operate according to these principles. Her example inspired others to believe in a God who desires that men and women should serve in his church as equals.

We read in William Booth's *Orders and Regulations for Staff Officers*, 'no woman is to be kept back from any position of power or influence merely on account of her sex'. In what is today a largely male-dominated movement, this policy is not always upheld; in fact, it sometimes seems that our attitude toward gender roles has regressed during the last 120 years. It is especially difficult for married female officers to attain leadership roles, as they are too often treated as secondary to their husbands.

**How can we encourage and appreciate female leaders
in today's Salvation Army?
Here are some practical steps we can take:**

1. When assembling leadership teams—for example, when selecting people to preach or lead worship in our church service—we should strive to achieve a balance between males and females.

2. Observe the composition of The Salvation Army's various governing bodies and be willing to voice your concern if they are excessively male-dominated.

3. Encourage female leaders; try to create an environment in which they can flourish.

4. Form a group that meets monthly to affirm young people as leaders and discuss matters of relevance to them. This may provide an excellent opportunity to encourage those who might not otherwise see themselves as leaders —including women.

5. Finally, men must allow women to lead. The Salvation Army is damaged when male egos cause us to exclude capable leaders from leadership roles.

chapter three:

Get Into Their Skins:

How Frederick Booth-Tucker revised
the missionary's job description

'We put our Salvation clock half an hour faster than the other religious clocks in India by adopting native dress.'
Frederick Booth-Tucker

Frederick St George de Lautour Tucker, could expect a delightful life. At 28 years old, newly married, handsome, intellectually gifted, scion of one of British India's most prominent families, he was virtually guaranteed both a brilliant career in the Indian civil service and the universal esteem of his peers. However, only a year later his career would be over, he would be arrested and imprisoned, and Bombay residents would see him walking barefoot through the city's most destitute neighbourhoods, holding a beggar's bowl. What happened to this young man? What force could derail such a promising life?

It all began with a Christmas edition of *The War Cry*.

Born in 1853 to English parents living in Bengal, Tucker came from a family that had long served with distinction in the far corners of the British Empire. His father was the ruler of a sizeable district, representing the Crown to hundreds of thousands of Indians and functioning as both a manager of public affairs and a magistrate. Frederick grew up in an atmosphere of dignity and authority, albeit one polluted by occasional reports of violent uprisings in other parts of the country. It was clear that not all of India appreciated British rule; still, the Bengali people held the Tucker family in high esteem. When the 22-year-old Frederick Tucker returned from schooling in England, there was no question that he was destined for a successful career as a civil servant.

It was not only Tucker's stellar lineage that recommended him for this vocation; he had ably prepared himself for it. He was in the habit of rising at four o'clock each morning, at which time, working while others slept, he applied himself to the mastery of Indian languages. He not only spoke fluent Hindustani and Urdu, but also learned Sanskrit in order to access the tradition of Hindu philosophy. Enterprising, diligent, unfailingly honest and intimately acquainted with Indian culture, Tucker was ideally suited to his role.

The only problem was his aggressive Christianity. Tucker had become a devout Christian after hearing American evangelist Dwight L. Moody preach in London, after which he began studying Greek in order to read the New Testament in the original (in later years he was seldom seen without his Greek testament). Anxious to begin full-time religious work, he would have left the civil service immediately had it not been for the protestations of his family. Nevertheless, in his off-duty hours he evangelised incessantly, not only among Indians but also among British troops, to such effect that a minor revival broke out among the soldiers. Some authorities were uneasy with Tucker's conduct, but he defended himself assertively, pointing out that he did not use his official role for evangelistic purposes, and that what he did while off-duty was up to him.

However, this dualistic existence could not satisfy Tucker for long. Although in all his relationships he was unapologetic about his Christianity (including his marriage—in 1877 he wed Louisa Mary Bode, like himself a zealous evangelist), he still felt unintegrated. Specifically, he was frustrated at having to keep his profession discrete from what was really the great work of his life—bringing the gospel to India's 300 million people.

Tucker was also dissatisfied with the methods of the established missionary churches. Although he actively supported them, he saw that they failed to earn the attention or the trust of the Indian people. A cultural gulf separated British missionaries from their congregants. As one of Tucker's biographers observes, 'The average missionary, living under European conditions, was regarded by the people as a sahib, one of the ruling classes, the preacher of a foreign faith, the faith of India's conquerors.' Tucker searched for another way. He found one in the biography of a Jesuit missionary, St Francis Xavier, who had forged an effective ministry by living among the Indians as one of them. Reading Xavier's biography, Tucker saw that it was possible to preach the gospel to Indian people in an Indian way.

Embroiled in professional controversy and dissatisfied with the narrow scope of his evangelical work, in 1881 Tucker read in a London religious newspaper of a new Christian organisation, The Salvation Army, which employed unusual methods of evangelisation. Inspired, he sent a donation to the fledgling organisation. In return he received a special holiday edition of *The War Cry*, four pages long, featuring the following words from the pen of William Booth:

> IF YOU HAVE ANY CARE FOR YOURSELF YOU MUST DEAL STRAIGHT WITH THE PEOPLE. If you do not, they will perish, and then you will hear of it again. An account of your stewardship will have to be rendered. The eyes you look into now will confront you again, and those lips that are now silent while you speak will have an opportunity of speaking to you then. Oh, shall they reproach you with the bitter, never-to-be-forgotten reproach, of not having dealt faithfully with them, not having told them the truth?

It was a curious yuletide message, but one entirely appropriate to Frederick Tucker's state of mind, striking him as though it had been written expressly for him. He requested leave from the civil service and hastily chartered a boat for England. His objective was to attend a Salvation Army meeting and meet William Booth in person.

In this he was entirely successful. After a rousing service in London—replete with a fiery sermon by Booth himself—Tucker accosted the General, enthusiastically declaring: 'I want to join you'. Booth's reply was not the warm reception such a capable and devout man as Tucker might reasonably have expected. Booth was sceptical of the young gentleman's new passion, suspecting that it would soon fade. 'You have not seen enough of us to know what we are', he said. '...Discover everything about us for yourself, and then—!'

Happily, this frosty response did not dissuade the civil servant, who spent the next four months touring The Salvation Army's operations and studying its methods. Finally, his leave nearly expired, he reiterated to Booth his desire to enlist. Booth promised that if Tucker resigned from the civil service he would be accepted, and Tucker willingly did so.

He was enrolled as a Salvation Army officer, given the rank of major, and appointed to a clerical role at headquarters, working in the legal and candidates' department. Yet his sights remained set on India. It may seem strange today that Booth did not send Tucker there immediately, but The Salvation Army, as such, was then only three years old, and had established only minimal overseas work even in the western world. At that stage a mission to a hugely populous oriental subcontinent seemed daunting indeed. Tucker, furthermore, was still untested, and Booth feared giving him too much exposure too early, rather like an athletic coach who limits the playing time of a talented young rookie.

However, Tucker made an effective pitch for his idea, presenting to the General a plan of striking originality, simplicity and boldness. He maintained it was essential to approach the Indians from an Indian standpoint—a missionary had no business Europeanising his audience. As an added bonus, living in an Indian manner would cost significantly less than living in a European manner. Booth was entirely won over.

After briefly serving as commanding officer at Camberwell corps (where he found time to translate the Salvation Army song book into Hindustani), Tucker finally left for Bombay with his wife[1] and a company of four other officers. It was July 1882. With them aboard the *Ancona*—beside their uniforms and an assortment of musical instruments—was the Army flag Catherine Booth had presented to them at their ceremonial farewell. On their way they passed through the Suez Canal, where one of the party ('Sister Jennings', about whom little is known) became ill, and had to return home. Louisa Tucker accompanied her.

Thus, the party that arrived in Bombay on 19 September 1882 consisted of only four people, 'three of whom,' Tucker wrote, 'knew little more about India's peoples, history, and geography, or languages, than they did about those of Mars'. Had their number been

---

1. *Louisa had at first looked down on her husband's new vocation; later, she happily enlisted. Frederick's parents, meanwhile, were predictably dismayed at his leaving the civil service.*

multiplied by a factor of 100, they would still have disappointed the city's expectations. For weeks the impending invasion of a missionary 'army' had been a subject of heated debate in the local press. Particularly concerned were other British missionaries, who, hearing that the Salvationists planned to adopt Indian ways, worried that as a result whites might lose prestige in the eyes of the natives. They wanted no blurring of the distinction between Englishmen and Indians. One churchwoman wrote to a newspaper with prim disdain, 'I am dreading the Army coming to India, and I am sure that many more here agree with me.'

The Salvationists were nonplussed at finding a group of police officers waiting at their point of disembarkation, never imagining that this force had been stationed there in preparation for their arrival. The superintendent of police addressed Major Tucker, inquiring where the rest of the army was. At the reply 'There are no more', the policeman exclaimed, 'But we expected you to be a thousand strong!'

Four officers were enough to create a disturbance. Three of them paraded through the streets in simple wooden carts that Major Tucker dubbed 'war chariots', while the youngest officer, Lieutenant Norman, accompanied them on cornet. The next morning, to his surprise, Tucker was summoned to the police station. He was told that outdoor processions were not allowed; he and his comrades must confine their activities to tents or meeting halls. But the commissioner of police did not count on the legal expertise of Major Tucker, who, familiar with the Indian civil code, retorted that no such ordinance existed. Nevertheless, soon afterwards Lieutenant Norman was arrested during a meeting in a public square. Tucker recounts: 'He shared his cell with a European who had been arrested for being drunk and disorderly. Both were brought before the Magistrate next morning and fined, the drunkard one rupee, and the Salvationist 20, for the crime of blowing his cornet in a religious meeting.'

It was the first volley in a protracted battle between The Salvation Army and the local authorities. This battle, one author observes, 'was to have far-reaching results for the cause of religious freedom in India'. Other arrests followed. Tucker would eventually spend a full month in prison—unsurprisingly, for he was far from compliant with the authorities. When a police officer interrupted an open-air meeting, shouting, 'In the name of Her Majesty, Queen of England and Empress of India, I order you to disperse!', Frederick retorted, 'In the name of His Majesty, King of Kings and Lord of Lords, I command you to stand aside!' In the second week of his stay in prison he was told 'in a friendly fashion' that he would be released if he promised to stop preaching in the open air. He replied: 'If I had a rope round my neck and were going to be hanged the next minute, I would not make such a promise.' He returned to prison for another two weeks. He would look back on his month in jail as 'a time of rich spiritual refreshment'.

As an unexpected side effect of all this, the Indian people came to see the Salvationists as champions of freedom against autocracy. As in the 1885 trial of Bramwell Booth and W.T. Stead, legal trouble served to further The Salvation Army's aims. Babu Keshab Chandar Sen, a prominent Hindu leader, wrote to Tucker, saying 'You have been most unkindly and unjustly persecuted', and promising his sympathy and support—'in spite of wide theological divergence'—as 'the tribute which every man owes to God's persecuted servants'.

Support for the Army's work grew rapidly. Tucker exulted:

> At last the ear of India's millions has been unstopped in a way that we ourselves little anticipated—its eyes are turned upon us. We see and gladly seize the most magnificent opportunity for spreading Salvation that has ever been offered to any human beings...

Three days after Tucker's stay in prison, 10 more Salvationists were arrested. But the tide had turned; by this time the authorities were anxious to be done with the matter. The magistrate offered The Salvation Army freedom to hold processions on all of Bombay's streets, provided that they did not sing while in the Muslim district, as the police considered this practice highly dangerous. Tucker accepted. The right of Christians to hold noisy street processions was now protected under law, a significant gain for civil liberty in India. Furthermore, the various prosecutions that The Salvationists had weathered in their first months in India had earned them numerous sympathisers. Their mission was gaining momentum.

However, controversy still surrounded them in Bombay. Some worried that The Salvation Army's notoriously flamboyant methods would degrade Christianity in the eyes of the Indians, who, it was supposed, treated religious matters with extreme solemnity. For example, the Indian correspondent to the London *Times* complained in laboured, slightly hysterical prose (especially for a telegram):

> To proselytize the natives of India by clothing the solemn tenets of Christianity in an unseemly surrounding of vulgar buffoonery can but end in defeating its own object, as it will disgust the feeling of grave reverence almost universally experienced by the natives for all religious subjects.

For his part, Tucker believed that precisely the opposite was true. In his autobiography he writes of the Indian people:

> Their own worship is so much connected with incessant tom-tomming, enthusiasm and noise that they do not understand the advocates of quiet religion. Reality and sincerity of heart are to them intimately connected with a more or less loud and demonstrative confession with the lips.

The contradictory views of Tucker and the *Times* correspondent highlight the difficulty of summarising the religious attitudes of 300 million people. Still, Tucker is right to point out, as he does later in this passage, that in the traditions of Hinduism and Buddhism 'religion means self-denial.' Accordingly, 'to connect it with self-indulgence and then dress it in a foreign garb' was repugnant for most Indians. Tucker, recognising this, trained his officers to speak Indian languages and think in Indian ways. They wore Indian clothing, lived in Indian lodgings and ate Indian food. Following William Booth's maxim 'Get into their skins', they took Indian names (Tucker's was 'Fakir Singh'), and even painted Indian caste marks on their foreheads (in yellow, red and blue).

This strategy produced magnificent results. General Booth, remarking, 'The tidings from India are like a romance', sent more officers to help expand the work. In Delhi, a prince offered The Salvation Army the use of his estate. One Hindu leader declared, 'If The

Salvation Army cannot do anything for India, nobody can.' In some cities Tucker arrived to find that a Salvation Army corps had already sprung up.

Nevertheless, he was, as earlier, dissatisfied. Surveying the Army's great success in India, Tucker noted with frustration that the majority of new recruits had already been nominal Christians before enlisting—in other words, The Salvation Army was failing to convert India's non-Christian people. He decided that more extreme methods were required, and resolved that he and his officers would set out across India as 'fakirs,' religious beggars who were recognised and customarily welcomed among the casteless and those of low caste. This involved walking barefoot. 'Our English boots were the objects of the keenest criticism, even in the cities, and we soon began to realise that this badge of Western civilization would have to go,' Tucker wrote. It also involved carrying beggars' bowls and living on scraps of food. The Salvationists had already made a great sacrifice by renouncing their position as 'sahibs'; fakirism, however, took this sacrifice a step further.

In all of this, Tucker himself led the way. Criticised for taking his methods too far, he replied, 'I must cross the line to find where the line is, but I never ask others to do what I myself have not already done.' He travelled widely throughout India and Ceylon, so much so that the Indian press admitted its inability to keep pace with him. The *Indian Witness*, for example, noted: 'Colonel Tucker of The Salvation Army moves about so much and so rapidly, that he is reported from two or three parts of India at the same time.' He was often accompanied by one of his standout recruits, Arnolis Weerasooriya, a zealous young

The Booth-Tuckers in Indian dress.

Singhalese with a regal bearing, European habits and an unusually competitive view of Christian spirituality. He came to The Salvation Army after searching for 'someone who loves Jesus better than I do'. The first person he found whose piety excelled his own was a Salvation Army officer. Weerasooriya said to himself:

> A white man has discarded his usual dress, and adopted that of India for the love of Jesus, and to win the people of the East, whereas I, a son of the East, have discarded my native costume for that of the foreigner. How then can I say that I love Jesus equally well? I have found someone now who loves Jesus better than I do. Can I rest satisfied with taking a second place? Never!

No testimony more vividly illustrates the profound impression that the sight of a European in Indian dress made on the people of India. Weerasooriya soon enlisted as a Salvation Army officer, in which role his zeal, his innate dignity and grandeur[2] and his drive for self-improvement made him highly effective. Two years before his untimely death from cholera in 1888, he was appointed India's Chief of the Staff, Frederick Tucker's second in command. Many were alarmed by the idea of an Oriental supervising Europeans, but The Salvation Army insisted that race should not be a barrier to leadership—a commitment Weerasooriya amply justified, proving a capable administrator and particularly effective as a missionary to his own people.

While Weerasooriya was still a captain he accompanied Frederick Tucker into a village in the region of Gujerat, where they received an exceptionally cold welcome. The villagers told

2. Brahmins often mistook him for one of their own. Tucker recalls: 'If at a railway station he happened to go to the filter for water, high caste travellers would call out to him to warn him that the water was polluted.'

the two Salvationists that they did not want to hear them or know anything about them—in short, that the missionaries ought to continue on to the next village. Instead, Tucker and Weerasooriya rested beneath a nearby tree. A number of the village elders, remorseful at having dismissed the two evangelists so ungraciously, went to see what had happened to them. They noticed that, although an Englishman, Frederick Tucker wore no shoes—and this piqued their curiosity so much that they decided, 'We will feel his feet to see if they are soft like a European's or hard like an Indian's.' Quietly squeezing the recumbent Tucker's bare soles, they realised with horror that his feet were soft, unaccustomed to the heat and wear of Indian terrain. They imagined—quite correctly—that by forgoing shoes Tucker had exposed himself to severe pain, and they suddenly became aware of the extent of his sacrifice.

Tucker awoke shortly afterwards to find an assemblage of guilty-looking villagers surveying him in silence. Ignorant of what had occurred, he conversed with them amiably and was invited to dine in the village.

That night he and Weerasooriya held a salvation meeting, at the conclusion of which several 'seekers' came to the front, sparking a revival in the region that led to several thousand more conversions. Eventually Tucker wrote to Bombay for more helpers, and the revival spread even further. Looking back on the episode, he remarked: 'I preached the best sermon I have ever given while I was asleep!'

Effective though fakirism was, not all officers could handle its rigours. Some insisted on European lodgings, others required sandals on their feet, still others transferred out of India altogether. Some even died from the hardship—in 1887, while Tucker was touring Ceylon, his wife Louisa, older than him and more frail, fell ill and passed away (was 'promoted to glory,' in Salvationist parlance) before he could return.

The following year Tucker married again, this time wedding Emma Booth, second daughter of William and Catherine. In deference to the Founder's nepotistic wishes, he adopted the Booth name, and has thus passed into Salvationist lore as Frederick Booth-Tucker. The Booth-Tuckers served several more years in India before leaving to assume command of The Salvation Army in the United States.

By the time of his departure, Frederick had left an indelible mark on India, and, indeed, on overseas missions generally. Although he was not the first to adopt the peculiar methods— we have seen that he took his inspiration from an earlier Catholic missionary—he was nevertheless revolutionary by the standards of his day. At a time when missionary work was closely linked with imperialism, he came to India not in the guise of a conqueror, but as one of the people, speaking, eating and dressing like them. It was one of the most original and effective evangelism strategies in the annals of The Salvation Army, though its origins lay much earlier in Church history. Wrote the Apostle Paul, ' I am made all things to all men, that I might by all means save some.'

✦ ✦ ✦

Insane Challenge:

There are few finer examples of incarnational ministry than Frederick Booth-Tucker, whose work in India was guided by a principle that might be expressed as follows: our methods of reaching people should not be imported from our own culture, but created and tested within the context of the community we are serving.

This principle reflects Booth-Tucker's intense commitment to his mission, which he demonstrated even during the years he spent in an obscure clerical appointment. He used this period to prepare for the challenge ahead, studying Indian culture extensively. Similarly, when we engage in mission we should fully immerse ourselves in the mind-set of our new community. We must eat, sleep and breathe a culture if we are to incarnate the gospel in it.

Booth-Tucker was so committed to India's people that he rose at four o'clock every morning in order to study their languages. How are you preparing yourself for ministry? What sacrifices are you making?

Booth-Tucker was not only a dedicated evangelist, he was also a visionary leader, dissatisfied with nominal Christianity and demanding salvation results. Today, many of our recruits transfer from other churches, but if we have learned anything from Booth-Tucker's amazing story, we should also be striving to reach those who have never heard of Christianity.

When reaching out to a new group of people, ask yourself the following questions:

1. What do they eat?

2. What do they wear?

3. Where do they live?

4. What is their average income?

5. What might be preventing them from coming to faith in Christ?

To communicate Christ's message, it is often not enough merely to understand a culture; we may also be required to sacrifice cherished aspects of our own ways of life. Our challenge as missionaries is not only to live _with_ people, but also to live _like_ them—a sacrifice Booth-Tucker and many other crazy Salvos have been willing to make for the cause of saving souls.

chapter four:

The Maiden Tribute of Modern Babylon:

How The Salvation Army and the press

collaborated against child prostitution

> 'Our work is to deliver people by turning them away
> from their iniquities. That is a fundamental principle.
> But we want help in that matter from the government.
> We want our lawmakers to make just laws...'
> *William Booth*

One morning in 1885, at around seven o'clock, the bell rang at the front gate of The Salvation Army's headquarters on Queen Victoria Street, London. A housekeeper arrived to find a 17-year-old girl wearing an elegant red dress. She said she had arrived in the city only a few days earlier, after leaving her rural home in response to an advertisement for a general servant.

Upon arriving at her new place of employment, she found that she had been lured into a brothel.

The brothel-keeper forced the girl to wear the eye-catching silk dress, but stopped short of forcing her to sleep with the house's clients, believing that, like others before her, she would eventually assent on her own. Desperate to escape but uncertain of where to turn, the girl recalled attending a Salvation Army meeting in her home town. In her suitcase she found a song book with the address of the London headquarters printed on its cover. She decided to seek shelter there, and snuck out of the brothel at four o'clock in the morning, clad in her red dress and clutching her song book in her hand.

Like a ghost sighting, the sudden appearance of this girl alerted Bramwell Booth to the existence of an alternative world, secret and terrible, hidden just beneath the surface of ordinary life. Her arrival would commence one of the most explosive chapters in the history of The Salvation Army.

Bramwell, the eldest of William and Catherine Booth's eight children, had been made an officer when the Christian Mission became The Salvation Army in 1878. He became his father's second-in-command three years later, at the age of 25. The best-known photographs of Bramwell Booth show him as an older man, the clean-shaven second General of The Salvation Army, a statuesque figure with an alert gaze and a flair for dramatic attire—his uniform is invariably embellished with an ornate black cape or a full-length military coat, and sometimes with an embroidered cap; often a miniature portrait of William Booth is pinned to his lapel (as much, perhaps, a token of his own prestigious heritage as a tribute to the Founder). In the cap's absence we glimpse Bramwell's mop of white hair, which looks slightly tousled, as though caught in a strong breeze. His two memoirs, *Echoes and Memories* and *These Fifty Years*, reveal an urbane and attractively rational mind, combining his father's rhetorical panache with his mother's intellectual culture.

In 1885, however, Bramwell was only 29 years old, and decades away from writing his memoirs. He resembled his father more closely at this time than he would in later life, with a slender physique and a long black beard, and he possessed the energy and daring that William Booth displayed as a young evangelist. His wife of three years, Florence Booth (nee Soper), was then only 24. A Welshwoman, Florence had a moon-like face and an air of pristine innocence—one contemporary described her as 'fair, blue-eyed, serene'. She was drawn to The Salvation Army after hearing Catherine Booth preach in 1880. In her diary she wrote of this event, 'Conscious only of curiosity to hear a woman preach...as the meeting went on a new vision of life came to me.' At the age of 19 she assisted in opening The Salvation Army's work in France, and a year later married Bramwell, despite the protests of her father, a prominent doctor who considered The Salvation Army unsuitable for an educated person.

'Florrie' was compassionate and empathetic by nature. On General Booth's advice, she was placed in charge of a home for street girls in Whitechapel, East London. She first learned of the sex trade in England through stories told by these girls. Florence's naiveté was such that she found this discovery an appalling shock. Her writings reveal how intensely traumatic the experience was for her: 'How acute the contrasts in my life at this time. Such bliss at home, the purest love of husband and my darling baby...then suddenly these terrible revelations!' She related these stories to Bramwell, but, out of sheer incredulity, and in order to console his distressed wife, he refused to take them seriously. He wrote:

> Thinking of the miseries of these poor creatures, Mrs Booth cried herself to sleep night after night. She told me of the most harrowing incidents which had come to her knowledge. I tried to comfort her by suggesting that the stories were probably exaggerated; and the credibility of these folks was not to be trusted too readily, and so on. But, presently yielding to her entreaties, I said that I would look into the matter myself.

The discovery of the girl in the red dress confirmed Florence's reports. Although he found the story difficult to believe, Bramwell was forced to admit: 'There was the girl...and there,

'Fair, blue-eyed, serene' Florence Booth.

William and Bramwell, united in mission and grooming.

moreover, was the dress, obviously not such as a mistress would provide for a domestic servant'. The Booths launched an organised investigation of the matter.

Florence interviewed a group of teenage girls at the Whitechapel shelter, one of whom said she had been drugged by a strange man and awoke to find herself imprisoned in a brothel. After overhearing other women in the house saying that she was intended for the sex trade in Europe, she escaped in desperation, leaping to freedom through a window. Such stories horrified the Booths far more than the sheer prevalence of prostitution in England—they were aware of the industry's existence, but unprepared for the revelation that girls as young as 10 were often entrapped in prostitution through schemes ranging from conniving advertisements to forcible abductions. Worse, it was clear that these were not random or unusual occurrences, but part of a regular and well-organised traffic across both England and the Continent.

Catherine Booth had long maintained that most prostitutes were not in their profession by choice, an opinion that received increasing support as more information about the seduction of young girls surfaced. The problem quickly became one of The Salvation Army's chief concerns. Finally, Bramwell reached a moment of decision:

> I resolved—and recorded my resolve on paper—that, no matter what the consequences might be, I would do all I could to stop these abominations, to rouse public opinion, to agitate for the improvement of the law, to bring to justice the adulterers and murderers of innocence, and to make a way of escape for the victims.

To 'rouse public opinion' against the sex trade, Bramwell recruited the help of the fiery journalist William Thomas Stead, a renowned public figure and long-time friend of William and Catherine Booth.

The name 'W.T. Stead' seldom appears in print without the word 'controversial' closely preceding or following it. The son of a Congregationalist minister, Stead was a capable reader of Latin, an arresting prose stylist, and a stern moralist. He had the righteous fervour of John the Baptist, the impulsiveness of the Apostle Peter, and, moreover, the two physical attributes which no 19th century moralist could do without, namely a thick beard and a furious glare. He diagnosed his society as 'full of dead men's bones and rottenness' and prescribed harsh remedies, from restricted suffrage ('We shall yet suffer evil results from the extension of the franchise to ignorant men') to capital punishment, which he strongly supported ('Murderers must be disposed of').

In his earliest editorials he spoke out forcefully against prostitution, calling it 'the ghast-liest curse which haunts civilised society, which is steadily sapping the very foundations of our morality'.

However, like Bramwell, Stead was initially sceptical when confronted with the facts about child prostitution. He agreed to visit the Salvation Army headquarters, where an expert presented him with a summary of England's feeble prostitution laws and an account of the sex traffic in Europe. He was then ushered into an adjoining room, where a former brothel-keeper, Rebecca Jarrett, waited with three former prostitutes, all younger than 16.

One by one, Stead plied them with questions and listened to their stories. After a time the girls left.

There was a pause, and Bramwell Booth looked at Stead. There followed a brief exchange that would prove decisive for the history of The Salvation Army. In Bramwell's words:

> [Stead] was evidently deeply moved by what he had heard. It had shaken his vehement nature, and presently his feelings found vent. Raising his fist, he brought it down on my table with a mighty bang, so that the very inkpots shivered, and he uttered one word, the word 'DAMN!' This explosion over, I said, 'Yes, that is all very well, but it will not help us. The first thing to do is to get the facts in such a form that we can publish them.'

'The facts' would be collected by means of two audacious stratagems: by recruiting a Salvationist to infiltrate a brothel, and by actually purchasing three teenage girls, one of whom would be immortalised in a series of Stead articles—entitled *The Maiden Tribute of Modern Babylon*—and in the scandalous trial that followed. In fact, The Salvation Army and W.T. Stead would expose England's sex traffic using the very tactics of subterfuge and deception by which it was perpetrated.

Stead, the veteran journalist, demanded first-hand information before proceeding to publication. In order to examine the situation independently of the stories told by the Whitechapel girls, he and Bramwell risked sending a female Salvationist into a brothel for 10 days, where she posed as a prostitute in order to observe the establishment's operations at close range. The Salvation Army provided her with enough money to keep the brothel-keeper satisfied, and it appears that she successfully avoided all clients, although Bramwell writes that she did have 'some unpleasant experiences.'

Among these experiences were encounters with girls of 13 and younger trapped in a life of prostitution—the spy confirmed the worst that the Booths and Stead had heard. Further experiments followed. Stead himself bought two girls from an old procuress for 10 pounds each, both of them younger than 16. The girls had only a vague idea of what was happening until Stead, in accordance with his 'vehement nature', gave them a blunt, informative address that, according to Bramwell, 'thoroughly frightened them'. He consoled them with five pounds each and sent them away—traumatised, perhaps, but hopefully wiser for the experience.

However, it was not enough for W.T. Stead and the Booths merely to satisfy themselves of the truth of these stories; in order to effect a change they needed to convince the public as well.

Accordingly, Stead and Bramwell hatched a plan that Roy Hattersley describes as 'a form of investigative journalism which was a hundred years ahead of its time'. The plan was, simply, to expose the full horror of child prostitution by buying a girl and shipping her to the Continent, proving beyond doubt how easy it was to accomplish such a thing, and, by implication, how regularly it was in fact done. The story would then be publicised in Stead's magazine, the *Pall Mall Gazette*.

The Booths recruited Rebecca Jarrett to find someone who would sell them a child. As an ex-brothel-keeper, Jarrett understood the inner workings of the sex trade, and had the necessary contacts. Before purchase, the child's virginity would be certified by a professional procuress—this being, in the words of Bramwell Booth, 'one of the abominations necessary to such transactions'—after which she would be left alone with Stead for an hour or so. This would demonstrate how readily a girl could be bought and delivered into the hands of a strange man.

The next stage was to ship the child to the Continent. To prove that Stead had not taken advantage of the girl, a doctor would recertify her virginity, after which she would be taken to a Salvation Army outpost in France. Finally, the story would be publicised throughout England.

Before putting this scheme into action, Stead wrote an outline of it and sent it to a number of England's foremost religious authorities, including the Archbishop of Canterbury and the Bishop of London. He hoped not only to win their support for the plan, but also to protect himself in case anyone should doubt his motives: were he brought to trial, in his defence he could call upon no less a witness than the Archbishop of Canterbury.

The plan was finally put into effect in the summer of 1885. Throughout, Stead was fixated to the point of eccentricity on the trivial details of the scheme's execution, insisting that it be conducted in as realistic a manner as possible—excepting, of course, the final act.

First, Jarrett conspired with a procuress and a pimp to buy Eliza Armstrong, aged 13, from her mother. It was agreed that Eliza should be purchased for five pounds. But because Stead had heard that there was no demand for 'damaged goods', he required that Mrs Armstrong be given a down payment of three pounds, with the rest promised once Eliza's virginity had been certified. The procuress duly confirmed the girl's virginity, and she was taken to a brothel, where an inebriated W.T. Stead was waiting. He was so determined to play the seducer's part faithfully that, although a teetotaller, he had imbibed a whole bottle of champagne before the evening began, having heard that this was the customary prelude to such diversions.

Such was Stead's confidence in his own resolve that he apparently did not worry that his drunkenness might lead him to compromise the helpless Eliza, who was to be sedated with chloroform before her arrival. As it happened, however, the girl woke up when he entered the room. Whether he took advantage of her wakefulness to give her a stern lecture, like the one he had given to the previous two girls, is unclear. In any event, she was eventually transferred to a hospital, where her virginity was again confirmed—so that we may safely assert that W.T. Stead's honour triumphed over his vehement nature and an entire bottle of champagne.

Bramwell Booth met Stead and the dazed, befuddled Eliza at Charing Cross, where the girl was placed in the care of the superintendent of The Salvation Army's rescue home in Nimes, France. By the time she boarded a boat across the English Channel, Stead's story was ready for publication. 'The case was proved up to the hilt,' wrote Bramwell Booth. Although this particular girl was unharmed, the ease with which the sex trade was generally conducted could no longer be denied: an English girl had been bought for five pounds, left in a brothel with a stranger, and shipped to the Continent with little more difficulty than would have been met in buying a bag of groceries.

The Maiden Tribute of Modern Babylon was a title calculated to offend. By suggesting that Victorian Britain, which prided itself on its advanced morality, was regarding the issue of child prostitution as backward, exploitive and venal as the religion of Ancient Babylon, Stead touched a raw nerve in his society. His *Pall Mall Gazette* series turned a blazing spotlight on a world that England preferred to leave hidden in darkness. It was therefore easy for the anger of the British public, which initially burned against those whom Stead condemned, to turn against Stead himself. Eventually Stead, Bramwell Booth and Rebecca Jarrett would all be prosecuted for their actions, in a trial arising as much from the nation's resentment of those who had exposed its evils as from the real transgressions of the defendants.

The first *Maiden Tribute* article was published in July 1885, followed by three more in the weeks to come. Stead described the sex trade, and especially the purchase of Eliza Armstrong, in gruesome detail, renaming Eliza 'Lily' in order to protect her identity. Immediately a wave of fury swept across London. Bramwell Booth, immodestly but perhaps accurately, claimed that the series 'took the British public by storm in a way that can hardly be paralleled in newspaper history'. Its explosive power was owed partly to the credibility of the *Pall Mall Gazette*, which was not a sensational tabloid but a respectable newspaper, one with, in Bramwell's words, 'a high reputation for exactitude'. It was, in fact, 'a paper of tone and privilege, much patronised by clubmen'. Accordingly, Stead's descriptions could not be readily dismissed; readers were forced to acknowledge the reality of the sex trade and the ease with which it was carried out under England's present legislation.

In the spring of 1885 Parliament's upper house had passed for the third time a bill to provide greater protection for young women. The bill specifically aimed to raise 'the age of consent', the age at which a girl's consent exonerated her seducer. At the time this age—'wickedly and absurdly', in Bramwell's opinion—was only 13, whereas in other parts of Europe it was as high as 18. Catherine Booth asserted that this low age of consent revealed the 'moral obtuseness' of England's legislators. The bill had been defeated in its first two hearings in the lower house, largely on the curious objection that mature-looking young girls would exploit it to seduce and blackmail rich old men. With the bill in the lower house for a third time in the summer of 1885, the *Maiden Tribute* articles were timed to prick the public's conscience at a moment when legislative action was an immediate possibility. If the age of consent was raised, it would be easier to prosecute those who seduced girls like 'Lily'.

Capitalising on the furore created by Stead's articles, The Salvation Army ran a publicity campaign advocating the bill. On 18 July *The War Cry* published a 'Special Notice' imploring readers to support the 'Protection of Young Girls':

> A PETITION to the HOUSE OF COMMONS for the above purpose will lie for signature
> at the various corps' headquarters throughout the country for the next few days. All officers
> and soldiers are earnestly desired to sign it and to obtain as large a number of signatures
> as possible.

Within two weeks 393,000 names were amassed.

Meanwhile, Catherine Booth adopted Stead's tactic of taking her cause straight to the top of England's social hierarchy, but she outdid Stead, posting a letter not to the Archbishop of Canterbury but to the Prime Minister and to Queen Victoria herself, urging them to support raising of the age of consent. A member of Victoria's entourage replied on behalf of the Queen, stating in a bland and diplomatically phrased letter, that although she could not involve herself in Parliamentary affairs, Victoria did support the Army's crusade for the protection of England's young girls. Judiciously selected passages of this letter—that is, the most supportive passages—were read aloud at Salvation Army meetings across London.

The petition, a roll of signatures four kilometres long, was presented on the day the lower house considered the bill. It was transported to Westminster Palace on a wagon drawn by four grey horses, and escorted part of the way (musicians were forbidden while Parliament was in session) by a 50-piece brass band with 'three hundred female members of the Army in their well-known uniforms'. Eight officers carried the massive document on their shoulders, like a casket, and left it on the floor of the House of Commons.

The petition requested four reforms:

1. The age of consent for girls should be raised to 18.
2. Procurement for prostitution should become a criminal offence.
3. Police should have the right to enter and search suspected brothels.
4. Soliciting women should become a criminal offence[1].

In the end the first, third, and fourth requests were too radical for the House of Commons. However, perhaps as a result of this petition the lower house went beyond the upper house's recommendation that the age of consent be raised to 15, and on 7 August ratified by a vote of 179 to 71 a motion to place the age of consent at 16, while effectively outlawing brothels[2].

The raising of the age of consent was a major victory for Stead and The Salvation Army: their involvement had galvanised a timid lower house to approve and even strengthen a bill that it had twice rejected. Yet as the true nature of their publicity tactics came to light, they found themselves the focus of public outrage.

---

1. *This item was likely the work of Catherine Booth. Frederick Booth-Tucker writes of her views on prostitution: 'The paltriness of the efforts put forth to minimize the evil staggered her, and the gross inequality with which society meted out its punishment to the weaker sex, allowing the male participators to escape with impunity, incurred her scathing denunciations.'*

2. *Interestingly, this act of parliament also criminalised male homosexuality (though this was not at The Salvation Army's urging), and it was under this provision that playwright Oscar Wilde was arrested and sentenced to two years hard labour in 1895.*

W.T. Stead in the prison uniform he wore each year on the anniversary of his incarceration.

From the start, a degree of ire was directed against the agitators' methods. Bookseller W.H. Smith refused to sell the *Pall Mall Gazette* when Stead's articles appeared; and one member of Parliament, his sensibilities offended by the campaign, derided it as an 'enthusiastic spasm of virtue'—though he obviously considered it not unmixed with vice, for he asked the House of Commons to prosecute Stead for distributing obscene material.

Instead, Bramwell Booth, Rebecca Jarrett, and W.T. Stead were charged with child abduction under an 1861 act that had never been used to prosecute real child abductors. A trial became inevitable when Mrs Armstrong, criticised by her neighbours for selling her daughter (generally a frowned-upon practice), attempted to vindicate herself by claiming that she believed her daughter was entering domestic service. A public outcry followed. Bramwell, Jarrett and Stead suddenly seemed deceivers rather than activists.

A certain amount of wounded pride undoubtedly entered into this outcry. Stead's articles had not made the simulated nature of Lily's abduction explicit, and, unable or unwilling to generalise from the example of this particular case, radicals who had erupted over *Maiden Tribute* were now acutely embarrassed to find that the outrage had been staged.

Bramwell, Jarrett and Stead were indicted at the Old Bailey, London's main criminal court, in the autumn of 1885, on the charge of taking Eliza Armstrong from her parents unlawfully and against their will. A crowd of ruffians gathered to witness the proceedings— 'Every blackguard in London must have assembled in Bow Street while the case was before the magistrate,' wrote Bramwell—while respectable members of society, though appalled

Bramwell Booth, second General of The Salvation Army. Can you spot the Founder in this photo?

by the sex trade itself, primly denounced the Army's methods of combating it. 'It was impossible to disapprove of theirs,' Bramwell noted, with typically Boothian pragmatism, 'because they gave no hint of having any.'

General William Booth stormed against these persecutions with greater expansiveness:

> It seems to me more like complaining of the dogs that bark, in order to show the enemy is there, rather than of the wolves that bite! There ought to be some proportionate measure of concern as to the horrors they exposed...what I am most concerned about are the miseries and sorrows that have been made known!

The Archbishop of Canterbury was present to testify on Stead's behalf, but was not permitted to do so. Stead's precautions were no use now that society had turned against him.

The trial was most excruciating for Jarrett, whose cross-examination concerned not only her involvement in the 'Armstrong Affair' but her entire career as a procuress. She said the testimony was like having 'all my past wretched life raked up'. Jarrett, who had joined the Army less than a year earlier, was still intimately connected to the world of prostitution, and she felt obligated to her contacts there as well as to her comrades in The Salvation Army. She even lied in order to protect them. The result was a tearful, confused and often contradictory testimony that ultimately damaged the defendants' cause. Some felt that Jarrett was a victim of emotional bullying: 'The Attorney-General did his best to upset her', wrote Florence Booth. On the other hand, Jarrett's lawyer Charles Russell made an impassioned two-hour speech in her defence, moving the entire court to tears, including the judge.

In the end Jarrett was sentenced to six months' imprisonment and Stead to three, while Bramwell was acquitted.

Until his death in April 1912 (aboard the *Titanic*), W.T. Stead wore his prison uniform every year on the anniversary of his imprisonment, considering it a badge of honour. Rebecca Jarrett lived to be 87, advocating until the end of her life the rescue of displaced women in London.

Years after the trial it was discovered that Eliza Armstrong was not the biological daughter of Mrs Armstrong. Bramwell Booth speculates in *Echoes and Memories* that had this fact come to light at the time of the trial, it would have significantly affected the outcome. Bramwell, of course, eventually became General of The Salvation Army, a role he held until shortly before his death in 1929. He reflected near the end of his life that while raising of the age of consent had been victory enough, the prosecution that followed was an excellent publicity campaign for the work of the Army.

> The trial did The Army a great deal of good. It made us known, and put us at one stroke in the very front rank of those who were contending for the better treatment of the lost and the poor; and while it roused some powerful enemies...the enmity lasted only for a time, while the

sympathy which was generated remained and remains a permanent possession. Our work for women was greatly furthered by these strange circumstances.

Insane Challenge:

Imagine being part of a campaign on the front page of a major newspaper—what was in the 19th century the primary media outlet of the day. How can we partner with today's media to expose injustices in our society?

The *Maiden Tribute* campaign grabs our attention for two reasons. First, the campaign was risky and highly publicised. Second, and most important, through this campaign the actions of just a few Salvos changed the laws of an entire country, which led to a reversal of fortunes for thousands of exploited girls.

We admire the willingness and determination of Stead, Jarrett and Bramwell, who didn't fear involvement in human trafficking, knowing that they had to expose the illegal trade going on in their day. They drew public attention to something harmful and degrading, something ignored by society and in need of change.

How can we achieve similar results? Today we are aware that humans are still bought and sold around the world, but fear risking our comfort or our reputation by taking action. We would do well to remember Catherine Booth's words: 'To better the future we must disturb the present'. If we desire change, we must be prepared to face opposition and criticism.

The Salvos discussed in this chapter were not afraid to violate the law in order to expose a problem that had to be addressed. Such daring protests are often effective in garnering media attention, which in turn awakens the public to the issue at hand.

The *Maiden Tribute* story is one of righteous anger, courage and innovation leading to justice for the exploited. As we combat injustices today, we can follow the four-step model used by Bramwell Booth and W.T. Stead:

1. Thoroughly research the issue.
2. Assemble a credible, competent team and develop a strategy.
3. Be willing to take risks, and, if necessary, put your reputation on the line.
4. Never back down—fight until reforms take place.

We are now facing the worst trafficking crisis in history, and we need to stand up and fight once again. Men, women and children are trafficked every day, both within their own countries and across international borders. Trafficking affects every continent and nearly every country.

www.stopthetraffic.org offers some disturbing statistics:

1. At least 12.3 million people are in forced labour worldwide. Of these, 2.4 million are victims of trafficking.
    (A global alliance against forced labour, International Labour Organisation, 2005)

2. 600,000-800,000 men, women, and children are trafficked across international borders each year. Approximately 80% are women and girls. Up to 50% are minors.
    (US Department of State Trafficking in Persons Report, 2005)

3. An estimated 1.2 million children are trafficked each year.
    (UNICEF UK Child Trafficking Information sheet, January 2003)

Some ignore the problem. Some acknowledge it, but reason that others can fight it more effectively. Some choose to take action—to stand up and fight. How will you respond? The choice is yours, but remember that the consequences of our choices affect the victims of human trafficking. We encourage you to act out of righteous discontent: fight for those unable to fight for themselves.

chapter five:

In Darkest England and the Way Out:

How William Booth fused
evangelism with social action

'It is one thing to press for action and another thing to know how and when to act.'
W. T. Stead

Thomas Henry Huxley, noted anatomist and spokesman for evolutionary theory,[1] was never shy of controversy. In 1860, publicly debating Darwin's theory at the Oxford University Museum, he responded to Bishop Samuel Wilberforce's jibe 'Do you consider yourself to be descended from a monkey on your mother's side or your father's?' with the retort that he would rather be descended from a monkey than from a man who used his talents to promote bigotry and distort the truths of science. At this, the audience erupted in mixed applause and shouts of complaint. In the ensuing tumult, Robert Fitzroy, the man who invited Darwin onto the *HMS Beagle*, now tormented by the thought that he had indirectly caused the literal truth of scripture to be discredited, was seen holding a Bible aloft and exclaiming 'The Book! The Book!'

Such religious fervour was always offensive to Huxley, who popularised the term 'agnostic' to describe his own views on religion. Unsurprisingly, he was a great opponent of The Salvation Army, never more so than when, 30 years after the debate with Wilberforce, General William Booth published a revolutionary plan for social reform entitled *In Darkest England and the Way Out*. It was not the details of the plan that offended Professor Huxley—although Booth's insistence that the reformation of society must begin with the

---

1. *He was also the grandfather of Aldous Huxley, author of* Brave New World.

individual soul's salvation certainly chafed. Rather, it was Booth's autocratic leadership style, the massive scale of the plan, and above all the prospect of a society run by religious fanatics, that so deeply distressed him. An aged man by this time, his huge sideburns gone entirely grey, Huxley responded to Booth's book in a series of furious letters to the London *Times*, documents of such virulence and bombast as to alienate even those most sympathetic to him. He likened The Salvation Army to 'a Sicilian mafia' and referred to the 'terroristic discipline and systematic espionage which my correspondents tell me is enforced by its chief'.

Although phrases such as 'terroristic discipline' and 'systematic espionage' tend to exaggerate William Booth's leadership style, there was nevertheless something of the dictator in the General; indeed, he was unapologetic about this fact. Had the recent book *Leadership Secrets of The Salvation Army* been published during William Booth's lifetime, it would have taken on a somewhat Machiavellian cast. As early as 1877, one year before The Salvation Army as such was founded, Booth had written, 'I am determined that Evangelists in this Mission *must hold my views and work on my lines.*' Other religious authorities tolerated Booth's style of leadership so long as his followers were only the officers and soldiers of The Salvation Army. When he sought to expand his sphere of influence to the whole of British society, however, he provoked the ire of men such as Huxley, for whom the Army was 'organised fanaticism' and Booth 'a despot'.

Booth was conscious of his own audacity, and in *Darkest England* he is at pains to show that his scheme is not intended for personal gain. He even qualifies the scope of its effect,

A General and a scholar.

noting 'I am under no delusion as to the possibility of inaugurating a millennium by my scheme.' Still, he does set forth a comprehensive plan for the alleviation of England's social ills—a bold enough endeavour, even when stripped of its millennial ambitions. He seeks nothing less than the total physical and spiritual regeneration of England's urban poor, and asks for the cooperation even of those who object to The Salvation Army's revivalism. Booth hoped that flamboyant uniforms and 'fanaticism' would not obscure the nobility of his aims:

> Look at that dark ocean, full of human wrecks, writhing in anguish and despair. How to rescue these unfortunates is the question. The particular character of the methods employed, the peculiar uniforms worn by the lifeboat crew, the noises made by the rocket apparatus, and the mingled shoutings of the rescued and the rescuers, may all be contrary to your taste and traditions. But all these objections and antipathies, I submit, are as nothing compared with the delivering of the people out of that dark sea.

Booth is offering what he believes to be an effective solution to the troubles of 'Darkest England'. His readers must either take it or leave it: 'The Plan has now been published to the world; it is for you to say whether it is to remain barren, or whether it is to bear fruit in unnumbered blessings to all the children of men.'

The 1890 publication of *In Darkest England and the Way Out* signalled a change of direction for The Salvation Army. It was an expression of William Booth's ideological transition from pure revivalism to revivalistic social reform. He remained unapologetic in his spiritual mission, proclaiming: 'I must assert in the most unqualified way that it is primarily and mainly for the sake of saving the soul that I seek the salvation of the body'; nevertheless, *Darkest England* was the culmination of a definite, if gradual, shift (what the official *History of The Salvation Army* calls 'the General's change of mind'). The fundamental Salvationist insight, 'What is the use of preaching the Gospel to men whose whole attention is concentrated upon a mad, desperate struggle to survive?' had flowered into an ambitious scheme that would place its author among the world's leading reformers.

The book's title employed a conceit similar to that of *The Maiden Tribute of Modern Babylon*, an alleged likeness between modern Britain and a distant, comparatively primitive world—in this case 'Darkest Africa', popularised by Sir Henry Morton Stanley's famous search for missionary David Livingstone.[2] The similar titles were no coincidence. The text of *Darkest England* was to some extent the work of W.T. Stead, who, at the very least, assisted Booth in distilling the final book from his initial compendium of ideas. Another important contributor was Commissioner Frank Smith, Commander of The Salvation Army in the United States, who influenced Booth's turn toward social reform and provided ideas and data for the book. The final text of *Darkest England* was really the product of three minds, even if its authorship was attributed solely to William Booth.

2. *Which, of course, ended with the classic greeting 'Dr. Livingstone, I presume?'*

The book was nevertheless a great accomplishment for the General, especially considering that it was published within a month of his wife's death. Created during the agonising year of Catherine's final illness, the work represented a triumph in the midst of suffering for both William and Catherine. Catherine, indeed, was an essential support to William throughout the writing process. He wrote in his preface: 'I do thank God she was taken from me only when the book was practically complete and the last chapters had been sent to the press.'

In light of the circumstances, it is remarkable that *Darkest England* is such a buoyant work, devoting a mere 76 pages to England's problems and 200 to their solution This solution is highly detailed and thorough, and, while utopian, is based on real experience— the book's first appendix outlines the work of The Salvation Army, enumerating the actual operation of several programs recommended in *Darkest England*. Moreover, while the book's proposed alterations to English society are extreme, the standard of living it seeks for individual Englishmen is modest. 'What, then, is the standard towards which we may venture to aim with some prospect of realisation in our time?' asks William, taking his cue from Thomas Carlyle. 'It is the standard of the London Cab Horse.'

'The Cab Horse Charter' is a phrase many Salvationists vaguely associate with the Army's storied past, without knowing to what it refers. Introduced in the second chapter of *In Darkest England and the Way Out*, it signifies the expected standard of living for a London cab horse, which, 'although a humble standard, is at present absolutely unattainable by millions'. There are two points in the Cab Horse Charter: 'When he is down he is helped up, and when he lives he has food, shelter and work.' The charter is the beginning of *Darkest England*'s transition from a depiction of England's social ills to an exposition of their solution. Although it appears early in the first part of the book, 'The Darkness', it offers a hint of the pragmatic confidence that characterises the second part, 'Deliverance'. It is the first such hint in the book; except for a few foreshadowing sentences, the entire first chapter describes the bleak present situation rather than a sunny potential one. Yet, in some ways, this exposition of the problem is the most important part of *Darkest England*. Whereas many of Booth's solutions were not adopted, at least not in the form he suggested, the attention he focused on England's poor made an immediate public impact.

The sufferings of the destitute ('the sons and daughters of misery', as one of his sermons designates them) excited William Booth's rhetorical imagination almost as much as his conscience. Some of his most memorable quotations are found in the opening pages of *Darkest England*, which refer to Greek mythology, the Bible, Dante and John Bunyan as well as Stanley's 'Darkest Africa'. London's poor districts are 'the great Slough of Despond of our time', as awful as Dante's Inferno, for 'the man who walks with open eyes and with bleeding heart through the shambles of our civilization needs no such fantastic images of the poet to teach him horror'. Certain passages emphasise the desperation of the times: 'Who can hope to make headway against the innumerable adverse conditions which doom the dweller in Darkest England to eternal and immutable misery?' Others emphasise the apathy of society: 'The exceeding bitter cry of the disinherited has become...as familiar in the ears of men as the dull roar of the streets or as the moaning of the wind through the trees.' A favourite motif is the inaction of the established church, which incurs the General's most furious indictments. In one memorable paragraph he virtually explodes:

> It is no better than a ghastly mockery—theologians might use a stronger word—to call by the name of the One who came to seek and to save that which was lost those Churches which in the midst of lost multitudes either sleep in apathy or display a fitful interest in a chasuble. Why all this apparatus of temples and meeting-houses to save men from perdition in a world which is to come, while never a helping hand is stretched out to save them from the inferno of their present life?

The outrage of this passage reflects William Booth's burning passion to assuage the present sufferings of others; because he worked tirelessly to this end, and because his passion itself arose from his Christianity, he had nothing but scorn for those who claimed to share his convictions while remaining politically unaware, apathetic or inactive.

What, then, does he suggest is the 'way out' of *Darkest England*? Any successful ameliorative plan, he insists, must meet several criteria. It must address both the character and external circumstances of the individual, be at once sustainable and immediately practicable, cause no harm and be on the same scale as the problems it opposes. Booth makes it clear in the first section of his book that the problems of *Darkest England* are manifold and widespread; his scheme, accordingly, is multifaceted and broad in scope—in his own words, 'a stupendous undertaking'. Its three primary components were the self-sustaining 'colonies' to be established in the city, in the country and overseas.

The City Colony would establish rescue homes for 'destitute men and fallen women', and, once their basic needs had been met, would provide them with factory work. Booth hoped that the Farm Colony would take in the surplus workers inevitably created by such a system, putting to use the 'vacant farms' found in 'almost every county in England'. Booth saw particular potential in the miles of unused land bordering the country's railroads, which, if cultivated, would not only provide work for those leaving the City Colony, but also provide food for those who remained. Booth's most striking idea, however, was the Overseas Colony, which would develop the 'millions of acres of useful land' that, according to the reports of Salvation Army commanders in Canada, South Africa and Australia, 'could be had almost for the asking'. Booth knew that staffing overseas farms with refugees from London's slums would strike some as outrageous. 'To mention Over-Sea is sufficient with some people to damn the Scheme', he wrote. It was the most daring proposal in *Darkest England*, and ultimately the least successful—unlike the City or the Farm Colony, the Overseas Colony was never implemented. It survives in a purely abstract form as a testimony to William Booth's sweeping vision. After the Overseas Colony, Roy Hattersley notes, 'Nobody could claim that *In Darkest England* lacked imagination or that its author lacked ambition.'

More successful were two chapters Booth seems to have added almost as an afterthought, 'More Crusades' and 'Assistance in General', which put forward widely varying ideas for social reform, including embryonic versions of modern institutions such as recycling, the Missing Persons Bureau and employment offices (two Salvation Army employment offices were opened in the year of *Darkest England*'s publication, 23 years before the first employment office was opened by the British government). Booth is less concerned with a systematic restructuring of British society than with individual programs for the solution of specific problems—for example, refuges for street children.

Many of his suggestions were remarkably progressive, especially those concerning prisons. Prisons, he declares, 'ought to be reforming institutions, which should turn men out better than when they entered their doors'; and yet 'they are often quite the reverse'. Booth proposes establishing a 'Prison Gate Brigade' to visit criminals while in jail. The brigades are to share the love of Christ, and, hopefully, diminish the prison's malign influence. Booth also accounts for released prisoners, proposing to meet them 'at the prison gates with the offer of immediate admission to our Homes', thus drawing them away from the pub—'where plans for further crime are often decided upon straight away'—and into a more wholesome community. The rehabilitated prisoner may eventually be employed in one of the three Colonies. If without a skilled trade, Booth pledges, 'we will teach him one'. Booth's insistence that the work of reforming prisoners begins 'where that of our prison authority ceases' set him apart from other reformers of his day. Hattersley even suggests: 'A hundred years on, that view is still regarded as dangerously radical.'

In Darkest England and the Way Out was published on 20 October 1890, 16 days after Catherine Booth's death. Detractors, noting Booth's acknowledgment of 'valuable literary help from a friend of the poor', claimed that the book was more W.T. Stead's than the General's, an assertion Stead denied vehemently in an 1891 letter to the newspaper *The*

Star: 'It is his scheme if ever a scheme was any man's, and although many were glad to help, the sole responsibility and dominating mind was his and his alone.' The book sold extremely well—10,000 copies on publication day, 40,000 at the second printing a month later, and, within a year, 200,000 copies. William donated all of the profits from its sale to the implementation of his plan.

The plan incited some controversy, but much more was incited by Booth's perceived megalomania—many accused him of claiming that his was the only possible cure for England's ills. Others objected to the General's militant, flamboyant methods. Of course, Booth had anticipated both of these criticisms in his text; nevertheless, for many the terrifying prospect of a Booth-governed, Salvationism-infused Britain outweighed the promise of the *Darkest England* plan. A London *Times* article appearing on the day of the book's publication observed:

> He has...displayed talent in disciplining and governing those who acknowledge him as their pontiff...But when Mr. Booth steps outside this groove of governing those of his own religious feeling, and making religious converts, to pose as the general regenerator of society, the world may be excused for feeling shy of his proposals...

However, there were others—some of them highly influential—who spoke more warmly of General Booth and his scheme. In a grand but stilted attempt at impartiality, Queen Victoria expressed her encouragement:

> The Queen cannot of course express any opinion upon the details of a scheme with which she is not yet acquainted; but understanding that your object is to alleviate misery and suffering Her Majesty cordially wishes you success in the undertaking you have originated.

The Bishop of Manchester, meanwhile, wrote, 'I am struck with the practical wisdom of your plan', but added a prescient cautionary note on the difficulty of the Overseas Colony. A certain Archdeacon Farrar preached a sermon on *Darkest England* at Westminster Abbey, and wrote an enthusiastic letter to General Booth:

> I have read with deep interest your suggestion of a systematic effort to deal with the mass of misery which exists in our great cities. So far as I am aware no scheme of the same magnitude has ever been proposed. I heartily wish that such an effort had originated in my own Church...

Another religious authority, Cardinal Manning, went so far as to claim that Booth's ideas had in fact developed in his own Church, albeit separately: 'Your comments on modern political economy, Poor Law administration, Government statistics, and official inquiries are to the letter what I have said in private and in public for years.' Finally, the actor Sir Squire Bancroft wrote to the *Times* with disarming candour, 'I know nothing of General Booth's scheme in detail, but it seems to me to be so noble in its object that something really serious and thorough should be done to aid it.'

Despite Bancroft's entreaties, *Darkest England* never gained the full support of organised philanthropy or the British government, and many of its ideas, including both the Overseas Colony and the Farm Colony, either failed to ignite or flickered briefly before dying away.

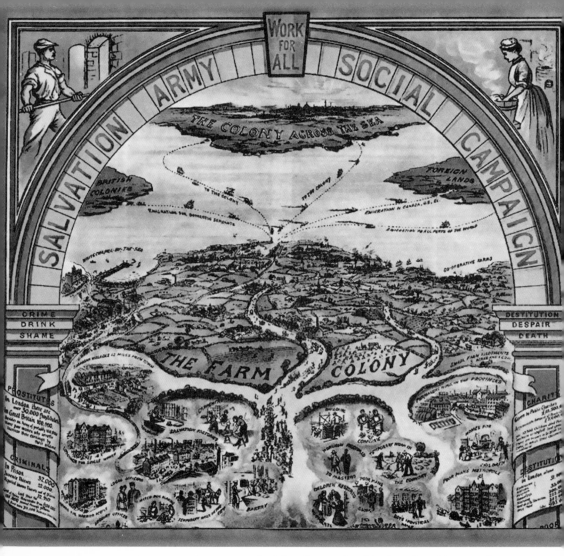

Booth literally mapped out his scheme for social regeneration.

Others, however, continue burning to this day. The rescue homes created as part of the City Colony still operate in cities around the world, and many of the innovations set forth in the final chapters of the book have been widely adopted. Edward Bishop, one of Booth's early biographers, asserts: 'There can be few families in Britain who have not been affected in some direction by the long-term results of the visionary proposals contained in William Booth's testament.' There was also the penetrating social critique with which Booth prefaced his scheme, a critique that, like the novels of Charles Dickens, brought the obscure squalor of London's slums sharply into focus for the British public. It was, all told, a monumental effort by the General, one which would both determine the future development of The Salvation Army and influence the attitudes and practices of an entire society.

✦ ✦ ✦

Insane Challenge:

Although William Booth's image of Victorian Britain was a painful one, it served to awaken his countrymen to the desperation surrounding them. Moreover, he not only drew a portrait of 'Darkest England', but also offered a comprehensive plan of 'the Way Out'. In this chapter we have attempted to convey something of the vitality of Booth's vision, but no mere summary could do justice to the passion, imagination and rhetorical force of his book. We recommend getting a copy and perusing its 276 pages for yourself.

Many of Booth's ideas are still applicable today. His concept of a 'colony' in which people meet one another's needs by sharing resources and community is still relevant and achievable. By working and living together, individuals can find comfort, healing and meaning—indeed, their lives can be transformed. In a day when many struggle in isolation, we need to create places in which Booth's dream of supportive community can be realised.

**Is there an idea from Darkest England that God
is prompting you to act upon?
For example:**

1. A refuge for street children
2. Prison reform
3. 'The Cab Horse Charter'—to ensure that all have work, food and somewhere to sleep.

It might also be worthwhile to take an 'In Darkest...' look at the area in which you live. This would require the following steps:

1. Gather statistics about unemployment, homelessness and other social concerns evident in your community.

2. Think creatively about how these issues can be addressed and write out (or, as Booth did, map out) a plan for a better future.

3. Share your ideas with local Salvationist leaders and political leaders (MPs, for example).

In his landmark work, Booth rebuked not only society, but also those churches that 'either sleep in apathy or display a fitful interest in a chasuble'. How would he address his own Army today? Are we asleep, or fully engaged in the fight to help those in need? Let's remain wakeful and carry out Booth's pledge to 'fight to the very end!'

chapter six:

Lights in Darkest England:

How The Salvation Army launched a
war on sweated labour and phossy jaw

> **'Born in slums, driven to work while still children,
> undersized because underfed, oppressed because helpless,
> flung aside as soon as worked out, who cares if they die or go
> on the streets, provided only that the Bryant and May
> shareholders get their 23 per cent?'**
>
> *Annie Besant*

The little-known Victorian musical *The Matchgirls* features a chorus of match factory workers chanting a macabre refrain:

> Phosphorous, phosphorous.
> Our special beauty cream.
> We look a proper dream—
> For we are minus a jaw.

A darkly humorous treatment of a gruesome reality. Phosphorous necrosis, or 'phossy jaw', was a famous malaise in the 19th century, a consequence of the poor working conditions in matchstick factories across Europe. The first reported case occurred in 1838. Marie Jankowitz, a matchstick-maker in Vienna, showed signs of corrosion in her jaw as a result of years of exposure to toxic white phosphorous vapours (white phosphorous was a common, but not essential, ingredient in matchstick heads). Her case was publicised in Austria's medical literature, and the country's medical community soon produced a small body of research on the disease. Although the reason for phosphorous' effect on the jaw was uncertain, it was discovered that the average time between a victim's first exposure and the appearance of 'phossy jaw' was about five years; of those exposed, however, only about five per cent were afflicted with the disease.

Phossy jaw clearly was not rampant in Vienna, but its symptoms were so devastating that the Austrian government launched an investigation into conditions in the city's matchstick factories. Improvements were recommended, but never implemented. Occurrences of the disease continued at a rate of around 10 per year.

Meanwhile, phossy jaw was attracting attention elsewhere in Europe. In France, a group of doctors observed 60 individuals afflicted by the disease, half of whom finally committed suicide in order to escape the agony of their condition. Phosphorous necrosis meant the decay of the teeth and jawbone, resulting in excruciating pain, disfigurement and the

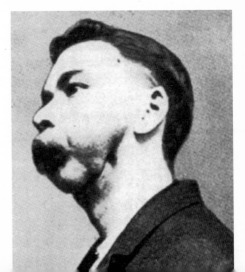

The ravages of phossy jaw.

suppuration of a fetid, oozing pus in the mouth—drainage from drying bone tissue—a discharge so vile that few doctors or nurses could be persuaded to treat it. In extreme cases it was necessary to remove the jawbone altogether, hence *The Matchgirls'* refrain, 'We are minus a jaw...'

English factory employees were especially vulnerable, as their working conditions were the worst in Europe. A prominent doctor visited a London match factory in 1843 and remarked that the atmosphere within was 'exceedingly disagreeable', adding that he was not surprised that the workers failed to complain, for many of them were only children, and, furthermore, they could earn twice as much working in match factories as they could elsewhere. The Queen's team of advisors ('Her Majesty's Most Honourable Privy Council') commissioned an investigation into phossy jaw in the 1860s, but, like the earlier investigation in Vienna, it produced no reforms. At the same time an article appeared in *Chemistry News* warning of the disease's effects, cautioning that those who dipped, dried, cut or boxed matches were at risk.

However, few of London's working poor subscribed to *Chemistry News*, and factory operators were indifferent. Thus, when The Salvation Army launched the 'Darkest England' scheme 30 years later, match factories were still dangerous and phossy jaw still a threat.

The character of the Army's work in this first phase of the scheme was as fearless and proactive as it had been in the case of *The Maiden Tribute of Modern Babylon*. As before, the Army identified an injustice in its community, carefully researched the problem and put a bold, practical solution into effect.

In 1891, under the direction of Colonel James Barker, The Salvation Army began investigating the conditions in England's match factories. Barker was amply qualified for the task. Ten years earlier, he had launched the Army in Melbourne, Australia, and had served as commander of 'all the colonies of the southern seas'. In addition to his great administrative experience, he displayed a positive genius for activism. One Salvationist writer notes that Barker would sometimes 'pace the floor with indignation against the conservative methods of Old England in regard to social reform'. His revolutionary prison gate ministry in Australia earned a citation in *In Darkest England and the Way Out*,[1] and he was so beloved in Melbourne that, when he received orders to return to England, city officials offered to finance him as an independent minister if he would stay.

Initially, phossy jaw was not The Salvation Army's major concern. In *Darkest England* William Booth condemned the 'sweated labour' system, which kept employees working in grim conditions for starvation wages, but it was chiefly low pay and not occupational hazards that attracted his ire. Discussing the 'City Colony' he suggested:

> Labour Shops will enable us to work out our Anti-Sweating experiments. For instance, we propose at once to commence manufacturing match boxes, for which we shall aim at giving nearly treble the amount at present paid to the poor starving creatures engaged in this work.

1. 'The right of entry into the jails has already been conceded to our people in Australia, where they have free access to, and communion with, the inmates while undergoing their sentences.'

However, Barker's study revealed that the problem ran deeper than paltry remuneration, iniquitous as this was. Throughout London's East End were factory workers showing symptoms of phossy jaw, and, despite the massive exposure required to produce the disease, its prevalence was hardly surprising. In one factory, Barker encountered a widow who with her two children, both younger than nine, spent 16 hours a day making matches. What is more, there could be no doubting the role of factory conditions in fostering the disease. At Bell and Co. factory, where matchstick composition paste was mixed on the roof, allowing phosphorous fumes to blow away, there had been only one mild case of phossy jaw in 50 years—whereas at the poorly ventilated Bryant and May factory the disease was commonplace.

The fact that Bryant and May was one of the safer match factories in England reveals how neglected factory workers were. Owners simply did not attend to the miseries of sweated labour and phossy jaw. Writes Robert Sandall: 'The big match-making firms of the day were fully aware of these evils, but callously refused to take any steps to remedy them, making no secret of the fact that they did so because it would have meant lessening the profits...' Only a public outcry on a scale sufficient to threaten these profits would alter their policies. Reformer Annie Besant proposed: 'Failing a poet to hold up their conduct to the execration of posterity, enshrined in deathless verse, let us strive to touch their consciences, i.e. their pockets, and let us at least avoid being "partakers of their sins", by abstaining from using their commodities.'

It was in this spirit that The Salvation Army planned to open its own match factory, which would pay more than other factories and produce only 'safety' matches, thereby eliminating the hazard of phossy jaw. A *War Cry* advertisement of July 1891 announced:

> 'Lights in Darkest England'—The Salvation Army Social Matches!! are now ready and orders can be executed forthwith. Everybody should use the 'Darkest England Safeties,' which are manufactured under healthy conditions and are entirely free from the phosphorous which causes 'Matchmaker's Leprosy'.

The Salvation Army purchased a derelict building in East London and converted it into a factory, paying workers almost twice what they received elsewhere: four pence per gross of matches versus two and a quarter pence—a significant improvement, even if it fell short of Booth's initial aim (to 'nearly treble' the rates of factory workers). But it was the elimination of toxic phosphorous from the composition paste that Booth emphasised at the official opening of the factory on 11 May 1891. He reminded his audience that no 'deadly white phosphorous' would be used, and urged them to show consideration for London's workers by purchasing only 'Lights in Darkest England' brand matches, made with a less hazardous form of phosphorous. The matches had been in production since April, and were sold in boxes imprinted with the Salvation Army crest, as well as a guarantee of 'fair wages for fair work' and a thematically appropriate salvation message (the promise of 'security from fire').

The Salvation Army ensured that the press was present for the factory opening, and the event received national newspaper coverage. The *Daily News* remarked:

> Whatever opinion may be held with respect to the religious propaganda of the Salvation Army... when it becomes widely known that there are not big dividends being wrung out of the makers of matchboxes bearing Salvation Army credentials, and that the matches are among the best in the market for money, there will most certainly be a rush for them, unless indeed, all the sympathy with a most helpless and unhappy class of workers for many years has been nothing but mawkish hypocrisy.

To further publicise the new factory's improvements in working conditions, Colonel Barker took a group of journalists and Members of Parliament into a factory where phosphorous-laden 'Lucifer' matches were produced. Extinguishing the lights, he let his guests glimpse the eerie phosphorescent glow of the workers' hands, faces and clothes. Afterward, the group toured the home of a family that worked in the factory, exhibiting the meagre conditions permitted by factory wages.

Of course, the Army did not hesitate to provide its own publicity. A series of advertisements in *The War Cry* touted the new initiative, using verse to achieve a memorable effect:

> The lights you purchased could not be but rank and shameful plunder,
> The outcome of the slavery the match-girls laboured under.
> So light no more your 'pipe of peace' with lights that but debase it;
> But let the sweating match work cease and noble work replace it.

Despite the *Daily News*' assertion that the Army's matches were 'among the best in the market for money', the relatively high cost of 'Lights in Darkest England' matches—nearly three times as expensive as other brands—made them difficult to sell. The Salvation Army did what it could to belittle this fact. One of Colonel Barker's investigators declared, with undisguised scorn, that the matches were 'cheap enough, surely', and suggested, 'If a man is not open to paying one farthing for a box of matches he ought to make them himself.' Happily, the Victorian era's spirit of reform momentarily triumphed over the spirit of capitalism, as many people were willing to pay extra in order to support the war on sweated labour and phossy jaw. The new venture's share of the matchstick market grew steadily.

The most important and lasting effect of this initial success was the attention it drew to the problems of the matchstick industry. Legislative results came in just one year—in 1892 the British government instituted new ventilation ordinances for factories producing Lucifer matches, resulting in decreased occurrences of phossy jaw. At the Bryant and May factory, for example, the rate of the disease shrank to around two cases per year.

Meanwhile, the commercial ascendance of 'Lights in Darkest England' was troubling the match-making authorities, and it was only a matter of time before they launched a counterattack. This finally came in the form of an inundation of Salvation Army safety matches available at the same price as ordinary matches—the market had been flooded with fakes produced overseas.

The Salvation Army responded by forming the 'British Match Consumers' League,' with members pledging to buy only safety matches produced in Britain under humane working conditions. Nevertheless, sales of 'Darkest England' matchsticks were now declining and the Army's factory of 100 employees had little hope of competing with major matchstick producers. Even in its demise, however, it drew attention to industrial corruption. Throughout the 1890s The Salvation Army tried various means of selling matches, advertising its virtuous production techniques, soliciting institutions rather than individuals and exporting to the colonies. Business remained unprofitable. The 'Lights in Darkest England' factory finally closed in 1900 and was purchased by Bryant and May.

By that time, however, the problems of the matchstick industry had undeniably entered the consciousness of the British public. An 1897 act of Parliament outlawed the employment of 'young persons in dangerous trades', drastically reducing the occurrence of child labour in British factories. In 1901 Bryant and May ceased using white phosphorous. Five years later, at an international meeting held in Switzerland, the production of phosphorous matches was finally outlawed.[2] Parliament responded accordingly, decreeing in 1908 that as of 31 December 1910 phosphorous matches would be illegal in Britain.

It was a belated reform (Finland, Denmark, and Sweden had all outlawed toxic phosphorous as early as the 1870s), but a reform nonetheless, and it was a triumph for The Salvation

2. 'The Berne Agreement' (as it was called) was signed by all countries in attendance—except the United States, which withheld its signature on constitutional grounds and promised instead to place a heavy tax on phosphorous matches.

Army, which in the face of both corporate and government indifference had successfully campaigned for improvements in England's factories. Although a commercial failure, the 'Lights in Darkest England' program revealed the difference that conscientious passion could make—provided, of course, that it received adequate publicity.

Insane Challenge:

James Barker was deeply committed to the cause of helping the last, the lost and the least. His compassion and righteous anger led him to respond actively to the injustices he witnessed in 19th century London. We, too, must be aware of the ways in which workers are exploited in our society, and look for opportunities to agitate for workplace reform.

Ask God not only to open your eyes to the needs of people in today's world, but also to give you a desire to help the oppressed (the fourth beatitude might be translated 'Blessed are those who hunger and thirst after *justice*') and the practical wisdom to aid them ('Be as shrewd as snakes and as innocent as doves,' Jesus enjoins us in Matthew 10:16).

As consumers, we can make a difference not only in workplace reform, but also in international trade. Combat economic injustice by buying fair trade products.

Better still, talk to your local café or supermarket and insist that they stock fairly traded products.

At its best, The Salvation Army has always acted as a voice for the voiceless. But while this voice has softened since the 1890s, oppression has not. We must speak out for those who are exploited in our day, just as we did during the 'Lights in Darkest England' campaign. If not us, who? And if not now, when? It is time for Salvationists to practise 'Aggressive Christianity' once again—to fight for justice, no matter the cost.

chapter seven:

Soldiers of the Cross:

How The Salvation Army took
Australia to the movies

'The magic power of light that can transpose pictures upon the film,
and reproduce them magnified upon a screen, is the creation of God,
and it can only honour Him, and glorify His own handiwork,
to utilise this invention for the salvation and blessing of mankind.'
The Victory, September 1901

H ad *Soldiers of the Cross* been written by Edgar Allan Poe and directed by Wes Craven, it could hardly have matched the violence achieved by Commandant Herbert Booth and Major Joseph Perry. As film-makers, at least, Australian Salvationists at the close of the 19th century displayed nothing of the fastidious aversion to physical realities that we generally associate with that era. In one of the film's milder scenes, we watch Christians being stuffed in bags and thrown in the Tiber river; at a certain moment we are privy to the stoning of Stephen, at another to Peter's crucifixion. One especially memorable sequence shows Christians being prodded into pits of burning lime. Although no footage survives today, all contemporary accounts and every extant photograph of *Soldiers of the Cross* indicates that the movie was a brutal one, a harrowing catalogue of the sufferings of the early martyrs, who are beaten, burned, beheaded, stretched on the rack and fed to lions, in the flickering glare of the silver screen.

The final frame shows Jesus gazing heavenward, and asks: 'Will you also follow Christ?'

Soldiers of the Cross, widely agreed to be one of the pioneering works of world cinema (precisely in what sense is a matter of debate), was not only a great innovation inasmuch as it was one of the world's first films; it was, as a film, astonishingly good—a compendium of simple, powerful images, surprisingly realistic sets and costumes and a cast of 'no fewer than 150', in Herbert Booth's estimation. *The War Cry* noted its effect on viewers: 'How deeply the emotions were stirred was evidenced by the involuntary interjections, moans of pity, sighs of relief.' The film's disputed status results from its unusual format. Although Australian film historian Eric Reade labels *Soldiers of the Cross* 'the first full-length film in the world', it was, by definition, not full-length (its reel length fell short of that standard by 2,000 feet), and even its status as a film is debatable. It was not a continuous movie, but a series of scenes, each no more than 90 seconds in duration, designed to illustrate Herbert Booth's oratory. At the premiere of Booth's presentation in 1900, *The War Cry* designated it a 'lecture'. However, it was obviously a lecture unlike any seen before.

> In the service of his Master, he had called to his aid the silvern tongue of eloquence, the divine power of music, the artist's scenic skill, and the still more potent incentive of the imagination, the cinematograph, enabling the living and moving tragedy of life to be portrayed before one's eyes, and had thus enchained the senses of his hearers, carrying them captive until his purpose was achieved.

This new medium, hailed as a more powerful 'incentive of the imagination' than rhetoric, music or painting, had entered The Salvation Army's evangelistic repertoire a few years earlier. In 1891 Major Alfred Barrett, touring the Army's prison gate home in Ballarat, Victoria, was intrigued to find a fully equipped photographic studio inside. It had been installed by the manager, Captain Joseph Perry, and featured a 'magic lantern', or 'limelight', used to illuminate photographic slides. Although photography was at that time only a hobby for Perry, he was obviously adept, for Major Barrett reported his discovery at headquarters, and the young captain was asked to bring his lantern to Melbourne, where he would use his skills to advertise the October visit of General William Booth.

Perry's work was immensely popular, and he was quickly appointed as 'creative artist and technician' in a new 'Limelight Brigade' to be directed by Major Barrett. Their first official presentation, on Boxing Day 1891, was a great success. Soon the brigade was touring Salvation Army corps across Australia, displaying photographs which increased in sophistication despite the demands of travel, as Perry introduced such devices as flashes of colour, brass band flourishes and split-screen effects to enhance his creations.

Five years passed, and a frail but energetic 34-year-old officer was appointed commander of The Salvation Army in 'Australasia' (Australia, New Zealand, Tasmania). It was Herbert Booth, fifth-born child of William and Catherine, a gifted songwriter[1] who, with his wife Cornelie, had come to Australia with exalted hopes. Three months after his arrival he published a 16-page manifesto in *The War Cry*, describing his vision of a mission to 'the multitude who march shepherdless and Christless to the grave from the luxurious lands that besprinkle the Southern Seas'. He continued:

> Who knows but that this first day of December 1896 shall be recorded in the annals of Australasian history as the day when there was started a crusade, which for deeds of holy

1. His hymns, such as 'Grace There is My Every Debt to Pay', remain popular among Salvationists.

Herbert and Cornelie Booth.

Joseph Perry: 'He was De Mille before his time.'

daring, for endeavours of whole-souled devotion, for acts of unflinching self-sacrifice, shall not
be outmatched by the valour of the Ancient Knights of the Holy Cross?

Under his administration the Australasian Salvation Army brimmed with creativity: he
initiated the construction of a new training college and printing press, increased circulation
of *The War Cry*, and founded a new periodical, entitled *The Victory*. These labours took a
toll on his delicate constitution, however, prompting his father to write in concern:

> Instead of responding to my suggestions that you should take it easy and get strong, you
> simply fill your letters with reconstructions and extensions and all manner of aggressions
> involving anxiety and toil which, if you were strong, would be delightful, but as it is, they sound
> to me calamitous.

But Herbert Booth was disinclined to rest. His imagination ranged incessantly over the
Army's operations in his territory, until it alighted upon the work of Perry, whose Limelight
Brigade, despite its relative venerability, was still only a small operation of one lantern and
300 slides. By this time, however, Perry had acquired cinematic aspirations. In August 1896
he watched the first cinematographic screening in Melbourne, a film of Australia defeating
England at cricket, and was struck by the notion that this novel technology could be used
to tell the story of the gospel. Booth agreed: if people were willing to pay several shillings to
watch an old sporting match, a screenplay would surely hold their interest. Booth bought
Perry a cinematographic machine, made by film pioneers the Lumiere brothers, and Perry
soon demonstrated his mastery of it, producing two short 'studies' ('Richard earning his

breakfast' and 'Wood chopping at the Metropole'), a brief documentary on The Salvation Army's social work in Melbourne, and a recording of the 1898 Salvation Army congress.

Emboldened by these early successes, Booth and Perry decided to direct their talents toward an uncompromisingly evangelical production, with Booth writing and Perry filming. Although the final product would obviously have high entertainment value, its explicit aim was to recruit '200 young male and female cadets' for the newly opened training college in Melbourne. It was to be a unique multimedia event, interspersing hymns, sermons and prayers with photographic slides and short film sequences. Booth and Perry selected as their subject the triumphant defiance of the early martyrs. They borrowed their title from a hymn to be featured in the presentation: 'Am I a Soldier of the Cross?'.

The film took 12 months to write and produce, as its creators took pains to ensure that it was historically accurate in every detail. It was filmed on tennis courts at the Salvation Army girls' home in the Melbourne suburb of Murrumbeena, which for a time swarmed with Salvationists attired as apostles and Roman centurions. A giant painted backdrop representing the Colosseum hung on suspended wires. Sometimes more elaborate contrivances were required to produce the film's effects. According to Perry's son Reg, who was 10 years old at the time of filming, the image of Christians falling into burning lime pits was achieved in the following manner: 'Dressed in togas and positioned on a raised staging, they were prodded by cardboard spears until they jumped—onto a mattress five feet below where a smoke bomb burned.'

Reg was given a unique role in the film, starring as the posterior of a papier mache lion, whose tail he controlled with a string (in *Soldiers of the Cross* a real lion roared at the Christians; a synthetic one ate them). His brother Orrie had the less ignominious task of manipulating the beast's eyes and lower jaw.[2] Meanwhile, Perry's youngest child, his infant daughter Edith, appeared as a babe in arms.

Burning was a favourite motif of *Soldiers of the Cross*, but a pressing concern during its filming was hypothermia. Behind the Limelight studios on Bourke Street in Melbourne, lightly clad actors were tied to stakes and left to shiver in the piercing wind. Even more hazardously, actual fires were lit beneath these actors, some of whom nearly choked on the resulting smoke. Beatrice Einsiedel, who played Nero's wife, recalled looking down on the

2. *One take was spoiled when the lion's hindquarters fell over. Its front legs subsequently attempted to right its back legs, but, alas, too late to save the scene.*

Slides from *Soldiers of the Cross*.

blazing fires and seeing the scorched hair and eyebrows of the actors. Clearly, there were certain risks associated with the production of *Soldiers of the Cross*. Happily, however, it appears that no Salvationists were harmed in the making of this film.

✦ ✦ ✦

The finished movie comprised 3,000 feet of film occupying 60 spools (coloured slides were used to hold the audience's interest while the spools were changed). It premiered on 13 September 1900, a night of inclement weather. This, however, did not deter hundreds of Australians from responding to the Army's typically flamboyant advertising.

TOWN HALL
This Evening 7.45 O'clock
WONDERFUL LIMELIGHT LECTURE
entitled
SOLDIERS OF THE CROSS
by
Commandant Booth

The audience was gripped from the first scene, a depiction of the stoning of Stephen. Later, the sight of an old man being thrown in the Tiber River—which bore a close resemblance to the local Richmond baths—earned a round of applause. To an audience largely unfamiliar with stories told in moving pictures, the effect must have been striking indeed. It was enhanced by Perry's film-making ingenuity, which, according to Reade, 'promotes

admiration, even today'. Reade claims that Perry 'covered huge crowd scenes with the dexterity of a seasoned producer', and goes so far as to call him 'De Mille before his time'.

That week's edition of *The War Cry* was even less restrained in its praise for *Soldiers of the Cross*:

> **It was a knock out.** Possibly 'knock out' is slang, but it is rapidly becoming good English, and we like to be a bit ahead of the times. In the pugilistic ring a 'knock out' signifies a victory about which there can be no doubt; which has been apparent to every beholder; which has satisfied friends, and even ill-disposed critics, if any were present. It is doubtful if there were any of the latter among the great crowd which assembled in the local Town Hall, notwithstanding the threatening skies.

In the view of *The War Cry*, however, the cinematic brilliance of *Soldiers of the Cross* was ultimately outshone by the nobility of its objective.

> The bold announcement by the Commandant that it was not his aim to entertain, but to rouse religious thought; that the object was not cash, but **to recruit cadets for Christ** may have come as a disappointing shock to some; but it at once raised the level of the lecture, and it was not long ere the lecturer had lifted his audience to the higher platform, upon which he had taken his stand.

Many representatives of the local press attended the premiere, attracted by the Army's promise of 'soul-stirring stories of the martyrs, illustrated by the most beautiful living pictures by cinematograph and limelight never before witnessed in this or any other country'. Their remarks, though naturally more guarded than those of *The War Cry*, nevertheless evince a high level of admiration. The *Argus* reported: 'Bold as the lecture was in conception, the illustrations were even more daring. Their preparation reflected the highest credit upon Commandant Booth and his assistants.' The *Age*, meanwhile, asserted: 'To have some of the most tragic episodes of Christian history carried out in all their savage but soul-stirring realism is an accomplishment essentially of today. It is a thrilling, novel and instructive lecture.'

The delirium of the premiere was only the beginning. Booth would soon present *Soldiers of the Cross* at packed venues in Sydney, Adelaide, Brisbane and New Zealand, sometimes earning as much as 120 pounds in a single night (then a large sum—the total production costs of the movie amounted to only 600 pounds). The film achieved such renown that Joseph Perry was established as one of the foremost film-makers in Australia, entrusted with the recording of such momentous events as Australia's first Federal Parliament and the visit of the Duke and Duchess of York.

Unfortunately, events soon transpired which would lead to the disappearance of *Soldiers of the Cross*. In February 1902 Herbert and Cornelie Booth abruptly left The Salvation Army, citing the movement's 'unjust, unreasonable and oppressive' chain of command in their resignation letter. Before departing from Melbourne, Herbert relinquished 300 pounds and the copyright to his hymns in exchange for *Soldiers of the Cross*, which he carried with him when he boarded the *Orizaba* on 3 September. For the next two years his lecture would be his primary, if not sole means of support. However, despite its importance to his livelihood, he apparently did not guard it very jealously, for somewhere along the way it disappeared. Later, Booth became a sought after evangelist in his own right, conducting successful campaigns in the United States, Great Britain, Canada and South Africa—but Australian film historians may never forgive him for his careless handling of his seminal creation. Of what once constituted *Soldiers of the Cross*, only a soundtrack and a few scattered slides can now be found.

Meanwhile, the indefatigable Perry continued filming, reprising his first great success with the remakes *Heroes of the Cross* and *Early Christian Martyrs*, and attracting capacity crowds to Melbourne Town Hall with the travel documentaries *In Sunny France* and *Amsterdam: Land of Windmills*. In 1908 the city's government selected him to film the arrival of the US naval fleet; in 1909[3] he had the distinction of making the first movie to star a dog. He left Australia in 1918 to commence evangelical work in Java.

The achievements of Melbourne's Limelight Brigade, particularly the monumental *Soldiers of the Cross*, now hold an established place among the most innovative evangelism strategies in Salvation Army history. Although the historical significance of Booth's and Perry's work has often been exaggerated, and remains debatable, there is no doubt that these crazy Salvos were among the very earliest pioneers of the cinema industry.

3. *But this was also the year in which a new commissioner, James Hay, closed Perry's film-making department. In his autobiography* Aggressive Salvationism *Hay wrote: 'The cinema, as conducted by The Salvation Army, had led to weakness and a lightness incompatible with true Salvationism, and was completely ended by me. This had affected at the time many aspects of finance, but within two years the income of every department was greater than ever.'*

✦ ✦ ✦

Insane Challenge:

The story of the Limelight Brigade offers another instance of Salvationists using innovative methods to proclaim their message. Once again, the Army was willing to take the gospel out of the sanctuary.

It all started with Captain Perry's 'hobby' of making photographs, which would surely not have reached its full potential without the encouragement of Major Barrett. What are we doing to support innovators in our midst? We must continue to seek them out and promote their work. Without its innovators, The Salvation Army will lose its identity and its effectiveness.

Herbert Booth supported Perry's growth as an innovator by purchasing a cinematographic machine. How can we put resources in the hands of our innovators? Often, we expect them not only to create new forms of ministry, but also to find independent means of funding them. If we wish to see our innovators achieve their best, we should be willing to assist them financially.

Commandant Booth envisioned *Soldiers of the Cross* as a recruitment strategy: 'The object was not cash, but to recruit cadets.' Like Booth, we need to ensure that our creativity serves the purposes of our mission. If we innovate merely to entertain ourselves, our work will be fruitless. Focused commitment to mission, by contrast, produces superb results.

Since 1900, movies have attained a prominent place in our culture. We should not let today's film industry dictate standards, but should commandeer this powerful medium to spread our message. We also have a potent communication tool in the internet. Like Major Barrett and Commandant Booth, we should look for and encourage new mission-related uses of the latest technologies, including blogs and other websites such as YouTube, Facebook and MySpace. Unless we are able to capture the attention of the people, our Army cannot march forward.

chapter eight:

Hamodava:

How The Salvation Army

put the tea in 'charity'

'There's nothing like an Army cup of tea!'
John Gowans and John Larsson

Invented' would be too strong a word. Still, if it is true that 'there's nothing like an Army cup of tea', it is also true that there is something like the 'Tea League' William Booth formed in 1897—fair trade.

The Tea League arose as a result of The Salvation Army's rapid overseas expansion in the late 1800s. With a copious and consistent flow of money required to sustain the organisation's burgeoning programs, General William Booth was growing anxious about finances. He held a finance council with his leading staff officers, and the result was a letter in *The War Cry* from the General himself, in which he offered fundraising advice to corps officers and recommended that each soldier establish a 'Lord's Corner' in his or her garden. The 'Lord's Corner', in the words of historian Arch Wiggins, meant 'setting apart a corner of one's garden for God, giving him a tree, fixing up a beehive, planting some potatoes, letting Him have a chicken...or making something for which one had ability, selling it and giving him the profits'. In Booth's judgment, it was 'a beautiful method for raising funds to spread salvation'.

The third item in the letter was the Tea League. Booth urged his readers to join him in pledging to consume only tea sold by The Salvation Army; every cup of tea purchased would help support the movement's overseas work. He concluded with assurances of his fidelity to his own advice. 'I am giving the dear Lord at least a tenth of my own income. I have joined the Tea League, and fixed Him up a corner of my garden.'

The league eventually boasted a membership of over 43,000.

Meanwhile, Commandant Herbert Booth adapted his father's idea to his own context. On 13 March 1897 he published an article in the Australian *War Cry* touting the new 'Missionary Tea League'. Its epigraph read: 'Whether, therefore, ye eat or drink, or whatsoever ye do, do all for the glory of God'. Booth wrote:

> The rapid increase of our work amongst heathen nations, together with the remarkable opportunities for extension that lie right before us, and to which we feel God is loudly calling us, requires a large and immediate increase of funds. It has occurred to the General that a simple and effective remedy lies ready to our hand, by which our friends can amply supply our present need **without in any way further taxing their liberality**—namely, by simply uniting together to drink teas bought, blended and sold for the benefit of the missionary operations of the Army.

Australia was to have its own brand of Army tea, named 'Hamodava'—the Singhalese word for 'Salvation'.

Imported from Ceylon, the high-grade tea was blended by Salvationists in Melbourne and sold at a low price, for Herbert had pledged to supply 'the best teas at the lowest prices at which they can be purchased'. Staff-Captain Ashley Lamb oversaw its production. An 1898

Victory article on the Tea League features an interview with the 'genial and business-like' Lamb, who displays all the punctiliousness of a dedicated factory foreman.

'Your Hamodava appears to be going splendidly, Staff-Captain. I shall be glad if you will kindly answer a few questions of mine.'

'Certainly,' was the pleasant reply; 'I will if I am able to do so.'

'How many tons of tea are you selling per month?'

'I would prefer to put it in cups if you don't mind,' he said, pulling out a piece of paper, and calculating rapidly. 'Say as many as five and a half million cups have been sold in a month.'

'But could you not put it into tons? You must be selling at least two or two and a half tons each week?'

The Staff-Captain shook his head. 'I prefer to be cautious. You must remember that a considerable quantity must, of necessity, be in stock in the various colonies...'

A more flexible mind seems to have guided Hamodava's advertising campaign, which featured a host of whimsical cartoons and jocular slogans. Beneath a pair of toucans with beaks tucked into their chests, we read: 'Keep your bills down with Hamodava'. Elsewhere, above the caption, 'Hamodava satisfies the best judges', two wigged magistrates sip from steaming cups. One advertisement shows a hand clasping a burning match, and reads: 'Hamodava strikes the fire of desire in the mind of the buyer...and the buyer of this excellent brand of tea helps the Army to save the lost!'

The tea received additional promotion from a song competition in *The War Cry*. One contestant upheld the grand Salvationist tradition of rewriting 'Champagne Charlie',[1] setting to that tune the following words:

> Two women at the washing-tub
> For many hours had stood,
> Till one unto the other said:
> 'I'd like some beer I should.'
> 'No beer for me,' the other cried,
> 'And you'll agree with me
> That beer is nowhere once you taste
> The Hamodava tea.'

This was a relatively unambitious entry. Another song, set to the tune of 'We're Marching On to War', features verses detailing the preparation of a cup of Hamodava and a chorus extolling the tea's benefit to foreign peoples.[2] This entry's most intriguing feature, however, is its elaborate choreography, which the songwriter helpfully provides:

> The singers should form a semi-circle on the platform. The one in the centre should hold a big teapot with the words 'Hamodava Tea' written across. The end men should have the cream jug and sugar basin respectively, and the rest of the company, cups and saucers with spoons. One

---

1. *See chapter 10.*

2. *We have elected to omit this song, as the chorus features racial epithets now excluded from the canon of political correctness.*

may take the verses as a solo, or several may take them in turns. Everyone should stir with a spoon at the chorus; it adds to the effect if one or two sisters, dressed as waitresses, bring in the cups, etc., upon trays.

In addition to its quality, economy and charitable object, Hamodava was touted for its evangelistic utility. On 1 July 1899 *The War Cry* ran an article entitled 'For God's Sake Help Me!: The Story of a Cup of Hamodava'. It describes a penniless, desperate alcoholic who demanded a cup of Hamodava from a female officer. The officer, after attempting to explain to the uncomprehending man that she had no tea, finally left the pub in frustration, glancing disdainfully at his bawdy companions as she did so.

Moments later remorse gripped her: 'Was she not God's agent, and had not Christ commissioned her to help such as this man?' The rebuke was undeniable—and yet, curiously, the officer chose to delegate her commission. Seeing a fellow Salvationist (a 'soldier-lad') approaching, she described the drunkard to him and told him to bring the man of a cup of Hamodava tea.

The lad did more than this. After procuring him the refreshing Hamodava, he took him down to his comrades, who gave him a shake-down for the night, and, next morning, a triumphant band marched him along to knee-drill. He was quite sober, but very ill from the effects of drink. While the prayers and songs of praise were ascending to heaven, the young man broke down and wept like a child, and before the conclusion of that knee-drill he had claimed and received God's pardon.

Like other Salvation Army innovations, Hamodava was immediately useful in the cause of saving souls.

High-collar uniforms and Hamodava: a typical family tea.

The chief innovation of the Missionary Tea League, however, was its attitude toward plantation workers in Ceylon. The Singhalese name alone suggests that the Australian Salvation Army was singularly mindful of the tea's origins, and this is confirmed by such *War Cry* articles as 'Where the Tea Comes From' and 'On a Tea Plantation'. Unlike modern fair trade organisations, the Army's Tea League was not established for the purpose of benefiting farmers or plantation workers: its aim was to assist Salvationist missionaries. Nevertheless, the character of the Army's dealings with tea growers was exceptionally just Frederick Booth-Tucker had noted the plantations in *Darkest India*, his review of Salvation Army operations in India and Ceylon. 'In Ceylon alone there are nearly 300,000 Tamil coolies [low-caste workers] employed on the Tea Estates, besides hundreds of thousands more who have permanently settled in various parts of the Island.' 'On a Tea Plantation', printed in *The War Cry* on 13 February 1909, links the work of these coolies to Hamodava tea.

The article opens with a description of 'the lovely island of Ceylon', which 'hangs like a gigantic pear' in the Indian Ocean. It then narrows its focus to show us the lives of coolie labourers. The female workers, we are told, receive lamentably small wages—'from 2d. to 4d. a day'—but 'seem to be a most contented and happy people'. Their strength and bearing obviously impressed the author. 'Each woman has a round basket slung behind her shoulders, with a band passing over the forehead, this method of carrying loads accounting, perhaps, for their straight stateliness.'

The meticulousness of the workers and the natural beauty of the plantation also seem to have intrigued the writer. He indulges in transports of lyricism:

> The silence impresses one, so quietly, so quaintly the pickers move amongst the laurel trees, for it is delicate work, and needs concentration...Every plot, right up to the crests of the rocky hills, is cultivated, wherever a bit of earth or the sediment, always drifting down to enrich the fields, has a foothold, the roots of a tea plant have possession of it. They cling to every craggy spot, just as the grape vines do in the south of France, or the rice on the terraces of the Ceylon foothills.

He is perhaps too charmed by the setting, for he pronounces the planters' bungalows 'a little earthly paradise', and asks, 'how can they be otherwise, with this tropical luxuriance in fruit and flower?' By comparison to 'the eternal squalid drudgery of country life in Australia', he considers the life of a Ceylon tea picker 'an ideal one'.

Although this is perhaps an excessively optimistic view, there is no doubt that these tea plantations were more equitably managed and less oppressive than many of their modern counterparts. In this respect they benefited from the generosity of the Army, which, according to Staff-Captain Lamb, was committed to giving tea retailers 'as good terms, or better, than they can get anywhere else'.

Like The Salvation Army's match factory, Hamodava Tea was commercially viable for only a few years. It enjoyed a brief flowering, adding Hamodava Coffee and Hamodava Cocoa to its production lines (the resulting beverage triumvirate was advertised: 'Every penny profit of the Hamodava trinity goes to save the world'), and at one point Staff-Captain Lamb, still refusing to measure sales in tons, estimated that 'if cups and saucers were filled with tea made from the output for one year they would make three lines totalling 3,790 miles [6,064 kms] in length'. Eventually, however, competition from 'cheap, inferior brands' forced the Melbourne plant to close.

But the Army Tea League lived on, later producing the popular 'Our General's Tea'. Salvationists across the globe showed their support for this new brand by signing the following highly conditional pledge:

> In order to help the General and his great work I will, providing that it is to my liking, drink the General's Tea for a period of six months; the condition being that you must make it possible for me to procure the tea without difficulty.

'The General's Tea' came in an 'attractive enamel caddy' decorated with a picture of William Booth, who was shown sipping a cup of tea at Buckingham Palace with Queen Alexandra and the Dowager Empress of Russia. This meeting had occurred in 1909, three years before the General's death. A remark he made to the two royalties was reproduced beneath the picture: 'If I had 80 years more to live I should devote them to the same work and purpose as that to which I set myself in the 80 years gone by.'

Insane Challenge:

Just as William Booth challenged his officers to find new ways of raising funds, we challenge Salvationists of today to be proactive in financial matters. We should not allow habit to dictate that we run old, lifeless programs, especially if these programs drain resources from more vital aspects of our work. We should think of ourselves as Salvation entrepreneurs.

The Tea League was an innovative use of an already existing behaviour pattern, as The Salvation Army turned tea consumption into a means of supporting its mission. Tea drinkers had only to switch brands in order to lend support to a worthy cause.

As Salvationists, we ought to be mindful of the ethical status of our expenditures. We urge Salvos to purchase fairly traded tea, coffee and chocolate, both individually and corporately. By buying 'fair trade', we can take a stand against the economic exploitation that is rampant around the globe. One way to reinforce financial commitment to this cause would be to sign a pledge such as that signed by Salvationists who drank 'Our General's Tea'. Why not ask your community to pledge to purchase fair trade products—or go further by starting a fair trade 'league' in your area?

A truly INSANE Salvo buys from corporations with a conscience, corporations that remunerate their employees fairly. Let's put our money behind our mission by supporting ventures that value people and glorify God.

chapter nine:

Marching as to War:

How doughnut girls brought
hope to the trenches

> '**Salvationists seemed always to be with us in the front lines and trenches. There was gratitude and near disbelief that anybody cared to make existence a bit easier.**'
>
> *Private John O. Findlay*

S oldiers are dreamers,' wrote Siegfried Sassoon, 'when the guns begin, they think of firelit homes, clean beds, and wives.' Sassoon, who fought in the hellish trenches of the First World War, knew well the extremities of human suffering that conflict involved, from tedious hours of idle, anxious expectation to acute physical privation to the terrifying rush 'over the top'—what Sassoon called the 'flaming, fatal climax' of a soldier's life.

In the midst of this nightmarish world, The Salvation Army carried on its work. With the same imaginative vision that enables a sculptor to see artistic forms in a block of marble, Commander Evangeline Booth saw in the United States' entry into the war a golden opportunity for Christian service. She wired Washington to offer The Salvation Army's assistance to US soldiers in France, but the government declined, asserting that the military's needs were already met by the Young Men's Christian Association, the Knights of Columbus and the Red Cross. But Eva would not be deterred. She assigned Lieutenant-Colonel William S. Barker to travel to France, investigate the lives of American soldiers, and identify ways in which The Salvation Army could be of service to them. Her confidence in Barker's tenacity overflowed. 'If you want to see Barker at his best,' she said, 'you must

Evangeline served as Commander in the United States for 30 years.

put him face to face with a stone wall and tell him to get through it. No matter what the cost or toil, hated or loved, he'd get there.'

Meanwhile, Eva arranged a personal interview with John J. Pershing, General of the US armies. Pershing loved The Salvation Army, having received a letter of condolence from Salvationists after his wife and children were killed in a fire in September 1915. He had never forgotten what he called 'the Army's expression of sympathy'. His meeting with Evangeline was brisk and decisive. 'I want to send my army to France,' Evangeline said. 'I already have an army in France,' Pershing returned. The Salvationist, feeling that her interlocutor had overlooked her essential point, countered: 'But not *my* army.'

By this time Colonel Barker was already in London, discussing Evangeline's plans with her older brother, General Bramwell Booth. Upon receiving word that Pershing had authorised The Salvation Army to join the American Expeditionary Force in France, Barker cabled back: 'Send over some lassies'. Finances, however, now became a pressing concern. Eva borrowed $25,000 from a bank and wired Barker: 'Eleven officers are being dispatched at once.' Bramwell, meanwhile, agreed to loan his sister $100,000 from The Salvation Army's international treasury. He was persuaded by her argument: 'It is only a question of getting to work in France, and the American public will see that we have all the money we want.'

The composition of the first group of Salvationists to join the AEF was perhaps not what Barker had hoped, consisting of seven men and only four 'lassies'. But the team was of an excellent calibre, having been selected by Commander Booth herself. 'I felt it was better to fall short in quantity than to run the risk of falling short in quality,' she explained. Her challenge to the departing group was memorable and stirring. One lassie recalled: 'As she spoke, although I am very short, I felt myself getting taller and taller.' The expedition sailed for France on 2 August 1917.

Arriving in France, American Salvationists found their countrymen dispirited. Soldiers who had dreamt of great battles and feats of heroism instead found themselves toiling knee-deep in mud. The men were depressed and homesick, and were consuming so much French wine that their commanders welcomed The Salvation Army chiefly as an antidote to drunkenness. High-ranking officers cheered the new arrivals; but, in Barker's words, 'among the regular officers there was a rather pessimistic attitude' toward the Salvationists. Perhaps Wesleyanism seemed out of place alongside the nihilistic sensibilities of war; perhaps, also, the soldiers resented sharing space and sustenance with unhelpful humanitarian groups. Whatever their scepticism's cause, however, it soon melted away. The soldiers first observed that the Salvationists were flawlessly egalitarian. They never entered the officers' mess, attending above all else to the soldiers' needs, and as the army moved closer to the front, they travelled with the infantry, sharing their hardships.

Later, however, it was the double-edged sword of lassies and doughnuts that cut away the soldiers' resistance. When four lassies toured the encampment at Montiers in September 1917, the men there refused to let them leave. The girls purchased their freedom by offering

to replace one feminine charm with another—that is, their own company with baked goods. This proposal was enthusiastically accepted, but its execution presented intractable difficulties. How were they to make pies with no stoves or pans and only a small amount of flour, grease, baking powder and sugar? Ensign Mary Sheldon, a former 'slum sister', resolved the difficulty by suggesting that they bake doughnuts instead.

This suggestion met with a round of applause. Unfortunately, they still lacked one ingredient—eggs. Armed with a French vocabulary that did not extend far beyond *des oeufs*, the name of the missing item, Ensign Helen Purviance left the encampment for a nearby village. Some time later she returned in triumph. Now all that remained was to make the doughnuts. Sheldon prepared the dough, using juice bottles to roll it and pop out the doughnut holes, while Purviance kindled a small fire, so low that she could not stand up while baking. She recalled, 'I was literally on my knees when I fried those first doughnuts, seven at a time, in a small frypan.' Her effort was warranted. As the lassies cooked, the entire division of soldiers chanted, 'We want doughnuts!' The first soldier to taste the result was Private Braxton Zuber of Auburn, Alabama, who pronounced the cooking experiment a success. 'If this is war,' he said, 'let it continue.'

The doughnuts proved so popular that the troops regarded them as the unofficial symbol of The Salvation Army. The lassies were soon rechristened 'doughnut girls', and Commander Evangeline declared that the servicemen had succumbed to 'the winsome, attractive coquetries of the round, brown doughnut'.

Although the treat was easily made, delivery was a constant challenge. Salvationists positioned themselves as close to the front lines as was allowed, running, ducking and diving to avoid enemy fire as they carried hot doughnuts to the fighting troops. Commander Joseph Hughes drove a truck full of baked goods directly into a fierce melee, gripping the steering wheel in terror and squeezing his eyelids shut. The artillery company cheered his arrival even as they continued firing.

During another battle, a doughnut girl attempted to carry a soldier's boots and a tray of lemon cream pies across a makeshift bridge. The soldier, observing her wobbling, cried out in alarm, 'Drop the shoes! I can clean the shoes, but for heaven's sake don't drop the pies!'

The lassies were occasionally careless with things other than pies: one evening, two of them fired at a German aeroplane with a borrowed rifle (it was what historian Edward McKinley describes as 'a moment of laughing high spirits')—thereby exposing the position of their entire company, which suffered an artillery barrage for the rest of the night.

Happily, the morale-boosting effects of the doughnut girls' work compensated for such gaffes. Testimonies such as that of Marine Charles Kamp were common:

> We were in the front lines. It was as black as pitch and raining like the hammers of hell. We heard the sentry halt someone and when we looked it was two SA lassies carrying a milk can of coffee and some doughnuts. The girls were soaking wet up to their knees in mud.

The persistent kindness and self-sacrifice of the Salvationists at the front left a deep impression on the servicemen. After the war, some even decided to transfer from one army to the other. Fred Wilkes, who had fought with General Pershing in the Mexican war, later became become a full-time Salvation Army officer. He told a friend, 'When I saw the Sallies with their ever willingness to help a fellow in need and expose themselves to all kinds of danger...I knew there was something in my life I'd missed. I can't get The Salvation Army out of my mind.'

They found various ways of eulogising the Salvationists. Harold E. Negly, for example, honoured the 'little doughnut girl' in verse.

> I've done my bit for Uncle Sam,
> Three thousand miles away.
> I have had my fill of fighting,
> And I'm home this time to stay.
> I think they'd have to drag me in,
> For another such a whirl,
> But I'd wade through hell barefooted,
> For the little Doughnut Girl!

There were never more than 500 American Salvationists in France at any point during the war, but their influence, both on the lives of US soldiers and on the development of The Salvation Army, was profound and enduring.

✦ ✦ ✦

The guns finally stopped blazing in November 1918. For two hours after the cease-fire announcement, soldiers on the front lines waited to hear the declaration of armistice confirmed. When confirmation came, it was met with incredulity. One doughnut girl recalled, 'Slowly, almost unbelieving men lifted themselves from the ghastly trenches, stretched weary, cramped limbs...There was no hilarious demonstration, no shouting, no loud hurrahs, no blowing of trumpets.' In the minds of the men, the war was not yet over; and indeed, it had not ended for every army on the field. Salvationist efforts did not abate with the declaration of armistice. A Salvationist who spoke fluent German accompanied the American generals into the opposing trenches, acting as an interpreter for the commanders. Elsewhere, doughnut girls carried trays of doughnuts to soldiers who had, only hours before, been mortal enemies.

Salvationists remained with the Allied army of occupation until September 1919. In port cities across the United States, meanwhile, The Salvation Army prepared to receive homecoming soldiers. As they disembarked, servicemen found Salvationists dispensing food, information, stamped postcards and free telegrams. They were especially useful in helping soldiers and their family members locate one another.

In March 1919, future US President Franklin D. Roosevelt, then Secretary of the Navy, sent a letter to The Salvation Army:

> The Department desires to express the gratitude of the officers and men of the United States Navy for all the many good things you have done for them during the World War. Whether the country be in peace or at war, there is a very constant need for your services.

The magazine was more wholesome in those days.

These sentiments were echoed across the nation. Evangeline's confident prediction that 'the American public will see that we have all the money we want' was amply justified, as the overflow of support that followed the war gave The Salvation Army an unprecedented level of financial stability, accelerating its evolution from upstart mission to magisterial charity. Evangeline was personally decorated for her leadership of the wartime service, receiving a Distinguished Service Medal from President Woodrow Wilson.

Eva did not consider the Army's work in the trenches innovative. 'What more natural thing?' she asked. 'We have only done an old thing in an old way.' Others agreed. One US soldier observed that the doughnut girls' work was only superficially different from that of Salvationists in slums around the world. 'Salvos have always been popular among the homeless. Now we are the homeless.'

In a sense, then, the Army's service in World War I was merely one more expression of its fundamental mission. Yet it was an expression unique to The Salvation Army; no other organisation earned such a cherished place in the hearts of that war's veterans. For soldiers resigned to 'dream of firelit homes, clean beds, and wives', the service of the doughnut girls was an innovation of luminous brilliance.

✦ ✦ ✦

Insane Challenge:

Initially, the United States military did not welcome The Salvation Army's World War I services—but Eva Booth persisted in her entreaties until she won acceptance. The Army's unique wartime ministry was difficult to launch, but its effects were immediate. The doughnut girls swiftly became indispensable to the troops in the trenches. What ministries are you attempting to start? Are you persevering in spite of obstacles, or are you quick to give up on ideas that God has given you?

It is important that we be enthusiastic and prayerful as we look for ways of serving others; it is equally important that we use our intellects to guide us in this search. Like Eva Booth and William Barker, we should carefully investigate potential mission fields before sending people to serve.

An enduring hallmark of The Salvation Army has been its soothing presence in chaotic and catastrophic situations. People around the world testify to our movement's kindness during and after floods, fires, cyclones, terrorist strikes and wars. As our army marches into the future, we must continue to be available to people in crisis.

We should remember, however, that ministry to those in catastrophic circumstances requires both grace and resourcefulness. Like the doughnut girls, we must use our ingenuity to extend supplies like food, drinks, clothing and bedding as far as possible. Our challenge is to continually expand our mission in new and innovative ways, creatively adjusting to each situation with grace and wisdom.

chapter ten:

An Open Secret:

*How The Salvation Army invented
contemporary Christian music*

> **'If standing on my head and beating a tambourine with my
> toes will win a soul for Jesus, I will do it.'**
> *William Booth*

In his first press interview as General of The Salvation Army, Frederick Coutts mentioned the Army's need to 'keep in touch with people, go where they are, and speak their language'. A young reporter pressed the General for specifics. 'You mean going into coffee bars?' 'If the people are there, of course!'

'To use coffee bar music?' (The idea was scandalous in 1963.)

'Why not?' Coutts responded. And, perhaps to placate traditionalists, he added: 'That's our tradition—we employ the language and music of the people.'

This was certainly true of the early Salvation Army, in which pub anthems like 'Champagne Charlie' found new life as the soundtrack to testimony meetings. Thus the chorus 'Champagne Charlie is my name' became 'Bless his name he sets me free!', while the opening line 'I've seen a deal of gaiety throughout my noisy life' was transformed into 'I was a slave for many years, and conquered by my sin...' The practice of singing pub tunes in church outraged many Victorians, but William Booth famously defended it, echoing Martin Luther's question, 'Why should the devil have all the best tunes?' Salvation Army brass bands became a fixture of poor neighbourhoods in London's East End, Salvationists were commonly seen singing in pubs and seedy dance halls, and the opening of the Army's work in Sweden in 1882 was accompanied by a guitar-driven rendition of 'We're bound for the land of the pure and the holy'.

However, alongside the abstract tradition of 'employing the language and music of the people' there arose a concrete tradition of Salvation Army music, an entire library of Salvationist hymns, choral arrangements and settings for brass bands. This tradition had its roots in the Army's earliest beginnings. Many a young Salvo has stoically endured the glorious but seemingly interminable verses of 'The Founder's Hymn', 'O Boundless Salvation', or been instructed by the ferocious lines of George Scott Railton:

> Dare ye still lie fondly dreaming,
> Wrapt in ease and worldly scheming,
> While the multitudes are streaming
> Downwards into hell?

In some quarters, however, Salvation Army hymn singing was eclipsed by Salvation Army banding, which grew into one of the strongest brass band traditions in the world. Pieces such as Eric Ball's 'Star Lake' became perennial favourites for brass bands internationally, whether Salvationist or non-Salvationist. Salvation Army band music reached a pinnacle two years after Coutts' fateful interview, with the debut of Ray Steadman-Allen's epic tone poem 'The Holy War' at the International Centenary Congress.

The only problem with all this was that by the 1960s brass banding, while still greatly popular, could no longer claim to be 'the music of the people'. In the early twentieth century this role was usurped by jazz and the blues, and by the '60s, of course, rock'n'roll was ascendant. The erosion of banding's cultural currency—along with that of military paraphernalia generally—altered the Army's image: to the new generation, a once radical and dangerous organisation now appeared old-fashioned and dull. A scene from the 1950 Broadway musical *Guys and Dolls* shows a Salvation Army open-air meeting failing to attract attention, its preachers and bandsmen outperformed by a travelling watch salesman.

On the other hand, most churchmen hated the new music, dismissing it as vulgar, anarchic, lascivious and obscurely satanic in origin. Like Socrates, rock stars were accused of denying religion and corrupting the young. But when reports of the Coutts interview reached the Officers' Training College in London, the principal, a Canadian expatriate and former military chaplain (in fact it was future General Clarence Wiseman), was inspired to form a rock group among his cadets.

It was typical of The Salvation Army's autocratic structure in the 1960s that the Joystrings began with an executive command. A contemporary band biography, *Joy and the Joystrings*, suggests that the group was conceived in the mind of Commissioner Wiseman and birthed by an official minute. 'We'll form a rhythm group,' the principal is supposed to have mused aloud—and one imagines him in a dimly lit office, his feet resting on his desk—'Captain Joy Webb, you'll take charge.'

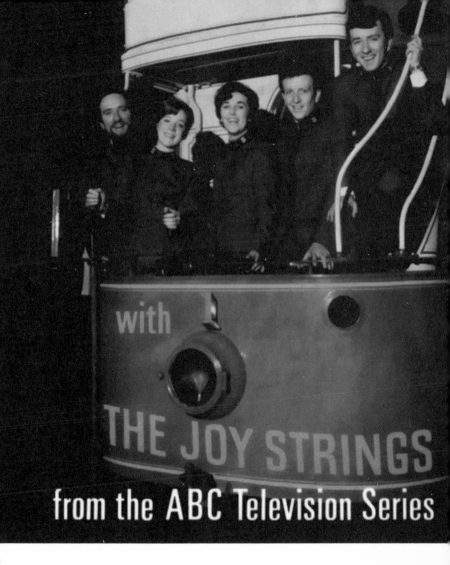

THE SONG BREAK

with THE JOY STRINGS

from the ABC Television Series

The Fab Five.

As a scion of a family of accomplished Salvationist musicians, Joy Webb was a sensible choice to lead the new group. Her father, a cornet soloist renowned for the purity of his tone, was first attracted to the Army by a percussion solo he heard at a concert in his home town of Coventry. He encouraged his daughter's musicianship, teaching her piano, vibraphone and fiddle, but thought it improper for a girl to play a brass instrument. Eventually Joy resorted to smuggling a French horn into her home. (Whether she actually played the instrument, and if so, how successfully she was able to conceal it from her father, is uncertain.) She sang her first vocal solo at age five, and later she and her father performed duets for cornet and piano. By the time she went to the training college, she was learning to play guitar.

In August 1963, Joy was no longer a cadet but a staff officer at the college. By this time, also— in the enigmatic passive construction of *Joy and the Joystrings*—'The Liverpool sound had been heard and the twist had been seen'. One of the new cadets was experimenting with this new sound. Peter Dalziel, recently arrived from Melbourne, Australia, had brought a guitar with him. Like Joy, he came from a musical family: his father was an expert on the concertina. It was a class of cadets rich in guitars, if not yet in guitarists: another new cadet, Bill Davidson, kept a little-used six-string gathering dust in his room.

At open-air meetings the cadets tried using guitars to attract listeners, but their skills were so rudimentary that few people responded. Nevertheless, when the official order came, the raw elements of a pop group were present. One evening Joy Webb invited all guitar-owning cadets to meet in the training college rehearsal room.

Peter Dalziel arrived, Australian guitar in hand, to find Joy with her new instrument (of indeterminate identity, it would later be recognised as a 'cello-acoustic') and a bevy of female cadets. Concerned by the absence of men in the group, Peter returned to his lodgings to persuade Bill Davidson to join. Bill dutifully wiped the dust off his guitar and made his way to the rehearsal room, now crowded with instruments. Indeed, this first rehearsal was something of an international guitar gallery. 'My guitar had never been in such a densely populated guitar area,' Bill recalled, 'there were a couple of Italian models, two Spanish-acoustics, a German-cello and an Australian model of questionable breed.'

At first the group was called 'The International Training College Rhythm Group', but, happily, they were later rechristened 'The Joystrings'—not, they insisted, in honour of their charismatic leader, but because their mission was to spread the joy of the Lord. The Joystrings' natural musicality was strong, but their instrumental prowess was weak. Initially, 'one or two chords' was the best they could manage. Nevertheless, excitement about the band spread so rapidly that the Canadian Broadcasting Company soon offered to record them. Thoroughly intimidated, Bill Davidson promptly resigned. Surprisingly, however, a second, even more daunting offer persuaded him to rejoin the group. Following the CBC, the British Broadcasting Company offered to record the Joystrings, and Bill realised that his meagre guitar skills would be required if they were to capitalise on their early success. A novice guitarist, Bill worked diligently to master the chords of G, C, and D.

After their performance at the BBC, recorded at a film site in an old block of Camberwell flats, letters poured in requesting further coverage of the group. The Joystrings had quickly acquired a following. One thing they still lacked, however, was a drummer. The group recognised that a beat group without a drummer was hardly credible, yet in order to find a competent percussionist they had to search outside the limited talent pool of the training college. A friend suggested Wycliffe Noble, a Salvationist from Liverpool (like Joy, Peter and Bill, his parents were Salvation Army officers), noted for his musical talent since his boyhood. In 1939 a weekly newspaper for Salvationist musicians ran a short notice on the precocious instrumentalist: 'Young People's Band-Member Wycliffe Noble, only son of Major and Mrs Charles Noble of Wealdstone, is making steady headway as a versatile percussionist.'

Wycliffe studied tympani and 'modern tone drumming' as an adolescent, but later decided against a career in music. He was launching a practice in architecture when the Joystrings contacted him in 1963. Nevertheless, he was willing to attend a Joystrings rehearsal, and made a powerful statement from the first song. In addition to his assertive drumming, his distinctive beard lent an aura of unkempt rebellion to the Joystrings' image, serving as a countervailing force to their buttoned-up high-collar uniforms.

The group soon recorded a 45 single and appeared on the 'Cliffe Michelmore Programme' and a 'Jimmy Young Saturday Special'. Their first live concert, however, did not come until March 1964, when they played at the Army hall in Lomond Grove, Camberwell. The concert had an energy, spontaneity and exuberance unusual for a Salvation Army gathering at that time, and at its conclusion hundreds of people came to pray at the altar. Joy Webb made it clear that the musical performance was less important than the message behind it. 'We don't want mere approval, or even support and appreciation,' she remarked, 'we need to make folk think, about themselves, about the world and about God.' The following week *The War Cry* predicted:

> Time will probably show that this meeting at Camberwell last Saturday night was historic, marking the first of a new kind of Army meeting—or is it a revival of an earlier kind, but in modern dress?

The War Cry recognised the similarities underlying the obvious stylistic differences between the Joystrings' Christian beat music and the early Army's Christian pub tunes. These similarities would be vividly reinforced when the Joystrings were invited to appear in a cabaret show at Liverpool's Blue Angel nightclub. Their decision to accept this offer incited widespread controversy—even the Reverend Billy Graham expressed his dismay. However, a Salvation Army commissioner, Samuel Hepburn, spoke in the Joystrings' defence, pointing out, 'The Army has been going into saloons, tap rooms, pool rooms and dance halls for scores of years, playing their music and singing their songs.' The Joystrings played a series of gigs at the Blue Angel, invariably taking the stage in the early hours of the morning. At the training college, several cadets set their alarm clocks to this time in order to pray for the group while they performed.

Although initially they had merely adapted old Salvation Army choruses, by this point the Joystrings were writing original songs. Their first hit was a composition of Joy Webb's, 'It's an Open Secret'. A sermon delivered by Commissioner Janet Wiseman, wife of the training principal, inspired the lyric:

JOY STRINGS

NO 'YEAHS' FOR ARMY

"**D**OMINIQUE," the smash hit by Belgium's Singing Nun, seems to have started something. Not to be beaten by sister Luc Gabrielle, and just over a month since "Dominique" dropped out, the Salvation Army group the Joy Strings make their initial entry!

The song, "It's An Open Secret," which makes its chart debut at number 29 this week, was written by the leader of the Joy Strings, Captain Joy Webb, in response to a plea made by the Salvation Army heads to carry a religious message to younger people through song.

"The thing was," says Captain Joy, "we had to go as near as we dared to commercial sounds—yet make the words crystal clear and see that it carried a certain amount of dignity. I mean we obviously didn't want anything which had 'yeah, yeah's' and 'woh, woh's' running through it!"

"It's An Open Secret" is the first single to be released on the Regal-Zonophone label for 15 years. The last was a Gene Autry disc way back in 1949. The label is now used exclusively for Salvation Army recordings.

The Joy Strings, four men and four girls, are on the administrative staff of the Salvation Army Training College

at Denmark Hill, except for architect-drummer Wyncliffe Noble. At first they had no plans to make a disc of "It's An Open Secret."

They featured it on BBC-TV's "Tonight" and the response was so great that they soon changed their minds and recorded the number.

And the record has certainly brought them plenty of chances to get their message across, for they are now in demand to make in-person appearances. One of their many commitments is a three-night stint at Mayfair's "Blue Angel" night club soon.

However, they are unaffected by their success.

"I know I'm a 'square,' but I still love classical music," says Joy. "But I listen to pop shows on the radio and TV and **try** to like that, too!

DAVID GILLARD.

STAR QUOTE

SURPRISING quote from Bobby Vinton : "Hollywood and movies were always synonymous with glamour and excitement to me. When I actually made a movie, however, I found it a dull experience. As a bandleader and singer, I've been appearing before live audiences since I was 15 and that's a lot more exciting and satisfying."

It's an open secret that Jesus is mine,
It's an open secret this gladness divine.
It's an open secret I want you to know,
It's an open secret, I love my Saviour so!

Joy Webb was not the only songwriter in the group. Peter and Bill composed another song, 'Love That's In My Heart', under decidedly exceptional circumstances. One evening, after 'lights out' had been signalled at the training college, the two cadets were struck with creative inspiration. Unable to play guitar or sing owing to the lateness of the hour, they worked out the tune quietly and surreptitiously, whispering to each other in the darkness, and finally set the words and chords down on paper. Bill considered the song's unusually complex structure a daring innovation. 'It was ahead of its time', he said. 'It had a key change in the verse.'

'It's an Open Secret' was released as a single on St Valentine's Day in 1964 (with B-side 'We're Going to Set the World A-Singing'), and reached #32 on the UK charts. That same spring, the Joystrings performed on the steps of St Paul's Cathedral to raise money for Third World needs. They played a variety of shows at this time, performing at Wimborne Minster in Dorset, at a Scripture Union Rally in Westminster Central Hall and at a public reception at Burlington House sponsored by the National Savings Committee, at which the Governor of the Bank of England was a special guest. Their popularity was so great that their performances often filled venues to the doors. When one rural corps invited General Coutts to speak, the corps officers added that a packed house would be guaranteed—if he brought the Joystrings with him.

By 1965 the Joystrings had become so popular that they were given a performance at the Salvation Army Centenary in the Royal Albert Hall, thus uniting in one program Salvation Army music's grand tradition (in the form of Steadman-Allen's opus) and its most contemporary expression. The presence of a rock group may have upset some congress delegates, but the Joystrings received enthusiastic support from an unexpected quarter— the July 10 *War Cry* noted that while the group performed 'the British Commissioner could be seen singing with them!'

In 1967 the Joystrings added 17-year-old guitarist Nigel Robson to their line-up, allowing Joy Webb to switch to organ. They played a number of live concerts and TV appointments in this year, and made recordings with Regal Zonophone, a division of EMI (a massive and eclectic label—EMI would later sign the Sex Pistols, among others). Compounded with the musicians' responsibilities as Salvation Army officers, this made for a gruelling existence. Even as cadets they had found the rock'n'roll lifestyle a challenge. Bill Davidson remarked:

> Life at the International Training College was…a strange mixture of study, examinations, and overnight train rides which took us from the windy quadrangle at Denmark Hill to the stifling heat of some far-distant TV studio. Monday would see us in the lecture hall and by Friday we would be, say, in Newcastle, playing to 2000 youngsters in the City Hall.

By 1967 the frenetic pace of life with the Joystrings was becoming almost unbearable. 'The Joystrings know what it is to work eight hours in the TV studios and realise only at the end how exhausted they have been during the last six of the eight hours,' Bill observed. The pressure was so intense that he even admitted:

> A tiredness overtakes not only the body, but the mind and spirit. Even the smile that has stamped the 'Joy' into the Joystrings is often difficult to find. I have often wondered when on stage what exactly I am so happy about, or at least why I should appear to be happy.

The group persevered until the summer of 1969, continuing to attract a sizeable following, and contributing all of their revenue to The Salvation Army. They recorded five EPs (including a Christmas EP, 'Christmas With the Joystrings'), and two LPs (both Christmas-themed: 'Well Seasoned' and 'Carols Around the World'), and, even more importantly, inspired an entire generation of Salvation Army pop groups. In fact, they predated other artists now considered pioneers of Christian pop music—Larry Norman, for example—and should accordingly be placed among the very earliest exponents of 'contemporary Christian music', now a massive industry. Later artists such as Michael W. Smith, dc Talk and Third Day can thus be seen as musical descendants of the Joystrings.

Just as remarkable is the group's association with an established church such as The Salvation Army. Ironically, the Joystrings belonged to what had become, 100 years after the Army's founding, an established tradition of innovation. Like William and Catherine Booth, George Scott Railton, Frederick Booth-Tucker, Bramwell Booth, W.T. Stead, Joe Perry and the many other Salvationists and Salvationist-affiliates discussed in this book, the Joystrings challenged convention for the sake of their mission. At a time when rock'n'roll music was literally demonised in many churches, The Salvation Army was willing to adapt the new sound to its own purposes—something Joy Webb and company accomplished with a prowess and flair that catapulted them from the training college and the meeting hall into the pop charts. Although the Founder could scarcely have imagined the direction Salvation Army music would take in the 1960s, one imagines he would have approved.

◆ ◆ ◆

Insane Challenge:

Music is a powerful medium, an international language addressed to the emotions, inspiring and challenging people of all generations. Most revivals in history have featured music prominently, and the rise of The Salvation Army was no different.

Brass bands were an especially effective tool for the Army when it began in 1878. Not only did brass music attract people's attention, it also inspired them to pursue the 'Salvation War'. The Salvation Army used the era's preferred music genre and favourite tunes; and, since brass instruments are portable, they helped the Army take the gospel out of the church and into the streets.

But while the mission never changes, our methods must continually change.

General Coutts, like William Booth, was willing to try new ways of reaching people, and his vision led to Joy Webb's forming a new music group that found receptive audiences throughout England. The Beatles and other rock groups were flourishing at that time, so The Salvation Army reinvented itself.

The impact was amazing. Once again the Army engaged with the major media outlets of the day, and since then Salvationists around the world have employed a variety of contemporary music forms to preach the gospel.

'Employing the language and music of the people' is a challenge we should be mindful of today. However, with the proliferation of pop music styles—from funk and rap to heavy metal—this is a more complicated task than ever before. We must continue to experiment, using different music styles to reach different people.

What, then, should Salvation Army music sound like today? It must be appealing, engaging, and, most importantly, life-transforming. Regardless of the style, unless it captures the attention of the public and draws them closer to Jesus, we are merely amusing ourselves.

We encourage the creativity and daring of today's Salvo musicians—we can redeem the 'devil's music', regardless of how loud or outrageous it may sound!

We conclude with a challenge for today's musically inclined Salvos:

1. Try uploading a music video clip on YouTube.

2. Take your musical group out of the meeting hall and into the community.

3. Rewrite lyrics to popular tunes (but don't break copyright laws!).

4. Set Salvation Army songs to new tunes—a good way to connect with people theologically and musically.

chapter eleven:

Insane:

How today's crazy Salvos are changing the world

'While women weep as they do now, I'll fight;
while little children go hungry as they do now, I'll fight;
while men go to prison, in and out, in and out,
as they do now, I'll fight; while there is a drunkard left,
while there is a poor lost girl upon the streets,
while there remains one dark soul without the light of God,
I'll fight—I'll fight to the very end!'
William Booth

In the introduction to this book, we asserted that 'the greater part of the INSANE story has yet to be written'. This holds in both a literal and a metaphorical sense: many stories of Salvationist innovators remain untold,[1] and many innovative deeds remain undone. Although we welcome a proliferation of sequels to this work, it is the undone deeds, the innovations still lurking in the minds of modern Salvationists, which interest us. If you have been inspired by anything you have read here, if you feel yourself impelled to action, put our book down immediately, write out your INSANE ideas and share them with an innovator you admire. This chapter ends with its introductory paragraph because the story it concerns is your life from this moment forward.

www.insanesalvos.com

1. *You may still be wondering, for instance, who 'Garabedian' is and why that little old bonneted lady adored Commissioner Andrew Miller. And then there is the loom on India's national flag…where did that come from?*

Bibliography

'An Argument for Hamodava', *The War Cry* (Australian), 10 December 1898

Baxter, John, *The Australian Cinema*, Sydney: Pacific Books, 1970

Begbie, Harold, *The Life of William Booth*, London: Macmillian and Co., 1920

Bertrand, Ina, Ed., *Cinema in Australia: A Documentary History*, Kensington, NSW:
        New South Wales University Press, 1989

Bishop, Edward, *Blood and Fire!: The Story of General William Booth and the Salvation
        Army*, London: Longmans, 1964

Bolton, Barbara, *Booth's Drum*. Sydney: Hodder and Stoughton, 1980

Booth, Bramwell, *Echoes and Memories*, London: Hodder and Stoughton, 1925

Booth, Catherine, 'Female Ministry; or, Woman's Right to Preach the Gospel', 1895

---. 'A Letter to William Booth, from His Fiancée, Catherine Mumford', 1855

Booth, William, *In Darkest England and the Way Out*, London:
        The Salvation Army, 1984

Booth-Tucker, Frederick, *The Life of Catherine Booth*, London:
        The Salvation Army Book Department, 1910

---. *Muktifauj: Forty Years with The Salvation Army in India and Ceylon*, London:
        Marshall Brothers Ltd

Chesham, Sallie, *Born to Battle: The Salvation Army in America*, Chicago: Rand
        McNally and Company, 1965

Collier, Richard, *The General Next to God*, London: Collins, 1965

Coutts, Frederick, *The Better Fight: The History of The Salvation Army*, London:
        Hodder and Stoughton, 1973, Vol. VI

---. *The History of the Salvation Army*, London: Hodder and Stoughton, 1986, Vol. VII.

Cox, Lindsay, 'Hamodava Tea', Australia Southern Territory Heritage Centre

Dale, Percival, 'The General's Tea', *The War Cry*, 2 July 1948

Dingman, Frances, 'Booth, Herbert (1862-1926)'

Emsley, John, *The Shocking History of Phosphorous*, London: Macmillan, 2000

Ervine, St. John, *God's Soldier: General William Booth*, London:
William Heinemann Ltd, 1934

Francis, William, 'Military Services: Doughnut Girls',
Historical Dictionary of The Salvation Army.

Gilliard, Alfred J., *Joy and the Joystrings*, London: Lutterworth Press, 1967

Green, Roger J., *War on Two Fronts: The Redemptive Theology of William Booth*,
Atlanta, Georgia: The Salvation Army Supplies, 1989

---. 'Booth, William.' *Historical Dictionary of The Salvation Army*

Hall, Ken G., *Australian Film: The Inside Story*, Sydney: Summit Books, 1977

Hattersley, Roy, *Blood and Fire*, London: Little, Brown and Company, 1999

Larsson, Flora, *My Best Men Are Women*, London: Hodder & Stoughton, 1974

Mackenzie, F.A., *Booth-Tucker: Sadhu and Saint*, London:
Hodder and Stoughton Ltd, 1930

McKinley, Edward H., *Marching to Glory: The History of The Salvation Army in the
United States of America*, Atlanta, Georgia: The Salvation Army Supplies, 1980

Merritt, John G., Ed., *Historical Dictionary of The Salvation Army*, Oxford:
The Scarecrow Press, 2006

'The Missionary Tea League', *The War Cry*, 13 March 1897

Murdoch, Norman H., *Origins of the Salvation Army*, Knoxville, TN:
The University of Tennessee Press, 1994

Ottman, Ford C., *Herbert Booth: A Biography*, Garden City, New York:
Doubleday, Doran & Company Inc., 1928

Reade, Eric., *Australian Silent Films*, Melbourne: Landsdowne Press Pty Ltd, 1970

Sandall, Robert, *The History of The Salvation Army*, London:
Thomas Nelson and Sons Ltd, 1950., Vol. I

---. *The History of The Salvation Army*, London:
Thomas Nelson and Sons Ltd, 1955, Vol. II

---. *The History of The Salvation Army*, London:
Thomas Nelson and Sons Ltd, 1955, Vol. III

Shirley, Graham and Brian Adams, *Australian Cinema: The First Eighty Years*,
Australia: Angus and Robertson Publishers, 1983

Tarling, Lowell, *Thank God for the Salvos: The Salvation Army in Australia, 1880-1890*,
Sydney: Harper and Row Publishers, 1980

Troutt, Margaret, *The General was a Lady: The Story of Evangeline Booth*, Nashville:
A.J. Holman Co., 1980

Unsworth, Madge, *Maiden Tribute: A Study in Voluntary Social Service*, London:
Salvationist Publishing, 1949

'Hamodava Unlimited: The Story of our Missionary Tea League', *The Victory*, 1898

Waldron, John D., Ed., *Women in The Salvation Army*, Oakville, Ontario:
The Salvation Army, 1983

Wiggins, Arch R., *The History of The Salvation Army*, London:
Thomas Nelson and Sons Ltd., 1964, Vol. IV

Dedication

To Herbert Booth (1862-1926),
a man who was certifiably INSANE,
and to all Salvo innovators—
including the ones who didn't make it.